BURPEE AMERICAN GARDENING SERIES

HERBS

BURPEE

AMERICAN GARDENING SERIES

HERBS

Martha E. Kraska

PRENTICE HALL GARDENING

New York ◆ *London* ◆ *Toronto* ◆ *Sydney* ◆ *Tokyo* ◆ *Singapore*

PRENTICE HALL GENERAL REFERENCE
15 Columbus Circle
New York, NY 10023

Library of Congress Cataloging-in-Publication Data

Kraska, Martha E.
    The Burpee American gardening series. Herbs / Martha E. Kraska.
        p.   cm.
    Includes index.
    ISBN 0-13-093709-6
    1. Herb gardening.   2. Herbs.   3. Herbs—Pictorial works.
    I. Title.   II. Title: Herbs.
    SB351.H5K73   1992
    635'.7—dc20   91-15735
                                                    CIP

Designed by Patricia Fabricant and Levavi & Levavi
Manufactured in the United States of America

10   9   8   7   6   5   4   3   2   1

First Edition

I would like to thank my husband, Peter Kraska, and my two sons, Todd and
Jonathan, for their encouragement and support. And a very special thanks to
Suzanne F. Bales and Edward Frutig for their invaluable advice and assistance.

I am also indebted to Burpee horticulturist Chela Kleiber and Burpee photography coordinator Barbara Wolverton.

Photography Credits

Agricultural Research Service USDA
Bales, Suzanne Frutig
Cresson, Charles O.
Fell, Derek
Kraska, Martha
Pavia, Jerry
Pavia, Joanne
Rokach, Allen

Line drawings by Michael Gale
Herbs in a Barrel garden design by Alice R. Ireys
Herbs in a Barrel watercolor illustration by Jean LaRue
Herbs in a Barrel design grid by Richard Gambier
Gardens shown on pages 15 and 18 designed by Nancy McCabe
Garden shown on page 12 courtesy of Mr. and Mrs. Gilbert W. Chapman, Jr.

On the cover: *A beautiful display of herbs at Boscobel Restoration Inc. in Garrison, New York.*
Preceding pages: *A circular herb garden featuring disease-resistant 'Simplicity' roses.*

CONTENTS

Introduction

Herbs are the most talented garden plants. They come to us as fragrances, culinary flavorings, insect repellents, medicines and dyes. It has been estimated that more than half of the medicines in use today trace their heritage to the roots, leaves, flowers and seeds of herbs. Herb history predates Christian times. Trial and error was the basis of research, and word of mouth the extent of communication. During the years of exploration to the Far East, the sailing ships that returned to England and Europe loaded with herbs and spices were most welcomed and their cargo most valuable.

Despite the many fascinating legends surrounding herb plants, our interest in this book will concentrate on the culture and use of those herbs that are culinary, aromatic and ornamental. These are the herbs that can make your life more enjoyable. Medicinal herbs, with all their superstitious or medicinal values, we leave to others. We'll start with the fact that many herbs are relatively easy to grow, far easier than the popular vegetables. Many are quite disease resistant, need little fertilizer and are tolerant of drought. They reward the gardener with a long growing season, providing flavor, color and fragrance well into autumn and winter. Most gardeners have grown some herbs, often without realizing that the plants are members of the wide-ranging herb family. Rose, foxglove and sweet woodruff are all attractive and useful members of this group.

Herbs are truly God's gift to weary gardeners. I first came to this realization a few years ago. I had always believed them to be mystical plants, something only a seasoned, mature gardener would attempt to grow. For years I tended a large number of gardens, all demanding endless hours of care and attention. As evening approached, after I had sprayed and pruned the roses, and limed and girdled the *Gypsophila*, weary and with a cool drink in hand, I always seemed to gravitate toward the herb garden.

Greeting me were the silvery blue foliage of rue, iridescent white-spiked *Digitalis*, Roman chamomile spilling onto the walkway and thyme running to and fro throughout the garden. I rejoiced to see my friends looking so well, and quickly asked myself if I had remembered lately to water or cultivate them. No need. The creeping thyme growing between the other herbs had kept its neighbors' moisture in and protected them from choking weeds. My friend rue, with its pungent fragrance, had kept those nasty little insects away, and their strong stems held them upright with no need of supports. All in all, they had tended themselves rather nicely. And sometimes, as a soft rain began to fall, I was aware of not only their visual beauty but of their wonderful, subtle fragrances. Herbs showed me just how durable, aromatic and decorative they truly are.

Put those durable, fragrant and disease-resistant herbs to use throughout your gardens. They are attractive, pleasing plants that will delight you and make wonderful additions to your landscape. Plant some herbs in your garden and enjoy their boundless versatility and lasting beauty.

Herbs are the plants that we have carried with us through the centuries, so often passed from grandmother to mother to daughter. These are the plants without which one never left home. They are a part of nearly every culture. As civilization spread to colonize new parts of the globe, the herbs always arrived with the first settlers.

An interesting mixture of textures is achieved by combining Nepeta, Lavandula, Nasturtium *and* Echinacea.

THE HERB GARDEN PLANNER

erbs are back. These talented, versatile plants are once again receiving the recognition they deserve. They are useful, attractive and extremely durable plants. Their demands are few: average soil, good drainage and sun. Some prefer dry, poor soil, while others prefer damp, rich soil, but most thrive in a wide range of soils and conditions. They are tough plants, some allowing you even to tread on them, then rewarding you with their wonderful fragrance. Combining usefulness and beauty, herbs deserve a place in your garden, and from there they will find a place in your heart.

An herb is any plant useful to man. This definition covers a broad range, of course. Some herbs reward you with flowers, whereas others provide wonderful fragrance and delicious flavor. In this book we describe more than 65 herbs. Some are tender perennials, among them scented geraniums, rosemary and pineapple sage. These will need winter protection in the colder climates. Others are hardy perennials—yarrow, sweet woodruff and mint, for example—that reappear year after year, dying back to the ground to return fuller and more vigorous each spring. Many of these herbs are prolific growers and will need division every few years to keep them in check. Other herbs are annual and biennial. Foxglove, dill and borage reappear every year, happily reseeding themselves. If you provide the right environment, biennials form colonies and spread happily throughout the garden.

Herbs come in a variety of heights, aromas and foliage textures. Some are a delight to the touch: woolly thyme, furry lamb's ears and velvety rose petals. Scented geraniums, sweet marjoram, rosemary and lavender are some that offer fragrance. Others bring the gift of flavor: mints, garden parsley, oregano, sage and many,

History of the Herb Garden

Herbs grown more than 2,000 years ago delight us today with the same wonderful aroma and flavor. If a time machine were to transport someone from the 14th century into a 20th-century herb garden, the time traveler would immediately recognize today's most popular herbs: basil, parsley, dill, chamomile, sweet marjoram, savory and thyme. Herbs are a living history.

Herb gardens are among the oldest of recorded gardens. Once the focus of every Roman garden, herbs are among the oldest cultivated plants. The Greeks were the first to introduce herbs into Italian culture many centuries ago. One of the first herbs brought to Italy by the Greeks was a rose, truly the oldest herb. Herbs thrive in the warm Mediterranean climate and most of the familiar herbs we cook with today are from this region. Planting an herb garden is a way for modern gardeners to reach back in time and share with the experience of people who lived more than 2,000 years ago.

Moonflowers and morning glories, both annual vines, enhance this herb garden.

many more are delicious additions to food and drink.

Health is another reason herb gardening is steadily gaining in popularity. Today there is growing interest in natural flavorings for better-tasting, healthier foods. Herbs are replacing artificial flavors and helping people cut down on the heavy use of added salt and sugar in cooking.

The renewed interest in cooking with herbs encourages better dietary habits that can lead to healthier and longer lives. People who cook with herbs are finding that good taste doesn't have to mean lots of fat and salt. You can avoid excess salt in your diet by using such herbs as sweet cicely, summer savory, thyme, lovage and sweet marjoram as "substitutes" in cooking.

If you've never grown an herb garden before, you'll discover a most pleasant experience. It can only leave you more knowledgeable, more skillful and a healthier, happier diner. It's sure to leave you a happier gardener.

HERBS IN HARMONY

The soft and subtle colors of herbs create a quiet harmony.

This artful blending of foliage colors includes garden sage, tricolor sage, basil and silvery thyme.

Herbs don't have to rely on the beauty of their flowers alone to give interest. Simply take a walk through an herb garden and you will be treated to a sensory delight. There are herbs with intriguing texture pleasing to the touch, pungent and invigorating in fragrance, and, of course, refreshing or rich in flavor. Combining plants with these diverse qualities in different ways creates a subtle, yet exciting, garden.

Each garden can be unique, with endless possible combinations of foliage color, foliage texture, flavor and fragrance. Try adding interest and harmony to your garden by blending different textures and colors. The variations in texture are many—the needlelike, sharp foliage of rosemary; the soft-textured, finely cut leaves of certain scented geraniums and the coarse, rough leaves of comfrey. Foliage comes in many sizes and shapes, too, from the large, finely toothed leaves of angelica to the smaller, soft, round leaves of nasturtium to the needlelike leaves of rosemary. All varieties in combination create a lush effect.

Try blending sweeps of various foliage color. Consider the light green foliage of lemon verbena woven around the vibrant, shiny dark green of germander or the warmer, gold-green of golden thyme. Imagine the blue-green–streaked foliage of tricolor sage as an accent for the silvery gray foliage of rue, southernwood or lavender. Shades of color woven together form an original garden tapestry.

Some herbs have foliage that remains evergreen throughout the year, providing winter interest. In February in my Zone 7 garden, after several snows, hard frosts and weeks of alternately freezing and thawing temperatures, the silvery foliage of rue and lavender, the deep green foliage of salad burnet and the shiny green leaves of germander persist. Some herbs take on an interesting seasonal color, such as creeping thyme with its burgundy winter coat.

As you might expect, some herbs offer even more than fragrance, texture and taste; they provide the added interest of flowers. While many of the herb flowers have inconspicuous blossoms, others provide a bonus of lusty or gentle color to your garden. Some of the more colorful and striking herb flowers are *Calendula*, with its sunny, brilliant yellow and orange flowers; the candy red flower of pineapple sage; the vibrant azure of the borage flower; and the subtle lavender-blue pompoms of the chive flower. These flowers provide further interest because of their various, distinct petal formations—daisylike flowers in the case of chamomile, globelike flowers of garlic chive, lacy flowers of dill and chervil.

HERBS FOR FOLIAGE

Angelica
Balm (lemon)
Basil (purple and green)
Borage
Chamomile (German and Roman)
Chervil
Comfrey
Costmary
Dill
Fennel
Feverfew
Geranium
Germander
Horehound
Lavender
Lovage
Mint
Monarda
Perilla
Rosemary
Rue
Sage (garden, pineapple, tricolor)
Santolina (gray)
Sweet cicely
Sweet woodruff
Tansy
Thyme (lemon)
Wormwood

FRAGRANT HERBS

Many of these herbs release their characteristic fragrance only when bruised.

Angelica
Balm (lemon)
Basil
Burnet
Chamomile
Dill
Fennel
Geranium
Hyssop
Lavender
Lovage
Mint
Monarda
Nasturtium
Rue
Sage (pineapple)
Sweet bay
Sweet marjoram
Sweet woodruff
Tansy
Tarragon
Thyme
Winter savory
Wormwood

Silvery thyme borders a vegetable garden.

Spilling out on a path are brilliantly colored nasturtiums, lavender and pansies.

In autumn, woolly thyme turns a burgundy color that stays all winter.

Sunny yellow Calendula *borders a showy display of* Allium sativum.

DESIGNING AN HERB GARDEN

Herb gardens are as varied as the tastes of those who create them. The size of your garden is entirely up to you, but I would suggest you start small, learning as you go which herbs thrive under the conditions you can provide for them. Start with a few culinary herbs, some hardy perennial ones like mint and oregano, then add some other easy annual ones—dill and parsley, and finally basil.

When designing with herbs, the first question to settle is that of location. Plant your culinary herbs where they are easily accessible to the kitchen. Try a fragrant herb garden near a patio or window where its aromatic pleasures can be most appreciated. Plant a formal knot garden where it can easily be viewed from a window or a porch.

After deciding where to place your garden, your next decision is which type of garden suits your needs and landscape. You can choose between formal (a

This small garden of culinary herbs is both functional and attractive.

Nepeta, lavender and artemisia in a formal herb garden.

knot garden surrounded by a low hedge) and informal (a gathering of the basic culinary herbs of chive, dill, parsley, basil, thyme, oregano and mint near the kitchen door). A classic, geometrically shaped herb garden divided into equal spaces, each filled with a favorite herb, is always a good choice because it is neat, attractive and an effective way to organize and display your herbs. Such a garden isn't necessarily formal, especially if outlined with old lumber or crushed stone, but you can create a formal look by using boxwood or brick walkways and adding a focal point like a statue or fountain. Some gardeners plant a collection of different members of the same family together as in, for example, a basil garden that includes cinnamon, 'Purple Ruffles', lemon, 'Green Bouquet', 'Green Ruffles', camphor, licorice and sweet basils. However you choose to arrange your garden, the important thing to remember is that the types of garden design are numerous and that there are no concrete rules.

Grouping herbs together in a garden looks and works well. But to fully appreciate the durability and beauty of herbs, try incorporating them into your entire landscape. Fill a pot or wooden barrel for the back steps. Use them to fill your window boxes. Stuff cracks in a walkway or staircase with creeping thyme or pennyroyal for both a lovely carpet effect and the wonderful fragrance they emit when trod on. Read on for some basic herb garden design forms.

A Circular Herb Garden

A circular herb garden is an attractive way to display your herbs. My herb garden is a rather formal one with a circular path of old brick surrounding it. The garden is divided into four pie wedges defined by bricks. The herb collection is housed inside the wedges.

In the center of the garden is a focal point, in this case a sundial. At the base of the sundial 'Simplicity' roses are planted. 'Simplicity' is a great rose variety not only for its beautiful pink color but because it is extremely disease resistant and grows well without the use of chemical sprays; dangerous chemicals are taboo around herbs and other edibles. Beneath the roses, lavender grows happily, emitting its pungent fragrance (a natural insect repellent). The roses and lavender create a pleasing partnership in the garden. The outer edge of each wedge is planted with alternating annual plants, parsley and marigolds. Using the same plants to edge each of the four beds visually holds the diverse four quarters together, giving the circular garden a finished look. The interior of each wedge is planted with combinations of different herbs. Every year this edging will change, always alternating two low-growing annuals. (Last year there were variegated nasturtium and curly parsley, and the year before, French marigolds and ruffled basil.) Thymes creep and scurry all about the bricks, weaving a path from one section to another.

I like to isolate any problem plants that would otherwise run rampant through the garden. Mints are especially troublesome, so pot the different varieties in large clay pots and place them about the garden. Mixing annuals with such "old reliables" as the perennial herbs lamb's ears, comfrey and bergamot can create a pleasing effect from year to year. *Calendula* planted in front of borage gave me a showy display of color one year, with the always-winning combination of yellow and blue. Last year my favorite combination was the brilliant red of pineapple sage with the almost metallic silver foliage of rue.

Every year has its surprises and indeed last year's giant angelica at 8 feet tall was one. (The plant description had indicated it would be 4 to 5 feet tall.) I was greatly pleased with its beauty but I had certainly not planted it in the right spot. Next year, I'll plan and find a better place, possibly in front of the fence where it can rise up and look over into the neighbor's yard. Little surprises like that are what make gardening so much fun. You never really know how a plant will perform until you try it in your own garden. That is why each year I like to try some different plants.

Last year, in contrast to giant angelica, a little gem entered the garden, an ancient Aztec herb called sweet herb (*Lippia dulcis*). It is a sprawling plant that sends out many runners. The small, rough-textured leaves cradle a tiny white flower that covers the plant all summer

long. When crushed, the leaves taste sweeter than sugar, thus its common name. It is not winter hardy so I potted up some in late summer to winter over on a sunny windowsill. This little herb proved to me once again that small is beautiful.

Formal Knot Garden

An old-world knot garden features elaborate patterns of variously shaped beds. In this type of garden, perennial dwarf hedges, for example boxwood, germander, *Santolina* and even lavender form the outline of the garden and its scrolling designs within providing interest throughout the year. These hedges act as backdrops for the herbs that "fill in" and keep the plants neatly in their place. Knot gardens are for the ambitious gardener who is willing to keep a close check on the hedges as they should be neat and well trimmed at all times.

Traditional Colonial American Herb Gardens

Busy colonists located their herb gardens near their kitchen door for convenience. Their herb gardens were simple in design and low in maintenance. The garden was often a square, divided into four equal sections for planting, and intersected by four paths of brick or gravel for maximum access to the beds.

Wagon Wheel

This early American design used the spokes of a wooden wagon wheel to divide herbs into beds.

A circular herb garden surrounded by old brick.

A formal knot garden.

It is an easy garden for a beginner. Search thrift shops and garage sales, particularly in farming areas, for a wheel; if you find a wheel without spokes, improvise spokes with metal strips. The eight wagon wheel spokes attractively hold eight basic culinary herbs. Sink the bottom of the wheel about halfway into the prepared soil and fill each section with several plants of the same herb. For a touch of whimsy use brightly painted wheels; try brick red, park-bench green or bright blue.

A mixture of assorted basils and flowering herbs in an informal herb garden.

Curly parsley is used to edge an ornamental flower border.

Herbs in Your Flower Border

Try planting some herbs into your existing perennial, annual or rose garden. This is a good way to grow herbs without creating a new garden. Plant some sweet woodruff, hyssop or parsley at the front of your garden; plant tansy, *Santolina* and coriander midborder and for a dramatic effect at the back of the border, angelica, aconite or lovage. Be daring! Herbs are not fussy and can thrive in a wide range of growing conditions.

Checkerboard or Terrace Gardens

The checkerboard garden is a very old garden design. Here, squares of slate or even crushed stones form a terraced area with planting pockets left randomly throughout the terrace. The stones act as a mulch that protects the plant roots from daytime heat and help to preserve moisture. This form of herb garden is also low in maintenance once the herbs are well established. Checkerboard gardens are good for small properties because they combine both a spot for entertaining and an attractive way to display your herbs.

Rock Wall Garden

A rock wall is constructed without mortar and provides spaces between the stones for the plants to grow. Fill the spaces with good soil, packed tightly to eliminate air pockets. Make sure the stones tilt inward so precious rain water will reach the roots of the plants. Use established plants with good root development; small seedlings can be washed away in heavy rains or dry out before they become established. Start planting from the top of the wall and work downward, squeezing the plants into their new home. Keep the new plants well watered until they are established. It is best to plant the wall in spring so that the plants have time to develop a good root system before the heat of summer. Many herbs love the conditions of rock walls. Try planting *Artemisia*, dwarf sage, *Santolina*, lavender, lamb's ears, creeping thyme and sweet marjoram. Once established, rock wall gardens are extremely easy to maintain. If you live in a northern area with cold winters, just be sure to check the plants in winter after an unusually warm day because freezing and thawing will often force them out of their pocket homes.

Courtyard Garden

My first real appreciation for herbs came about quite by accident. I had a much-traveled back courtyard, a sad area with three dirt paths, constantly used to enter my shed, workshop and garage. It was an ugly sight in every season, with no hope for a lawn. The idea of adding stones where lawn should be came to me. After removing the lawn and digging down 16 inches, adding some sand and lots of compost, I was ready to put in place the large, irregularly shaped stones. Pockets were left, large enough to hold low, spring-blooming bulbs and other plants including heaths and heathers. The first few months the new courtyard was in place left everyone a little cold, as many plants didn't do well. The traffic disturbed them and the courtyard once again looked grim. But I noticed that the plants that thrived were the herbs, so I planted more. By placing creeping thyme, lemon and golden thyme, garlic chives, low-growing rosemary, nasturtium, Corsican mint, wormwood, chamomile and *Nepeta* between the stones, I created a living carpet. The courtyard took on a new beauty. Herb plants proved hardy enough to withstand the constant traffic. I began to see a wonderful transformation. No question, the herbs were what this area needed; durable and tolerant, they flourished where other plants would not. As a special bonus, in my household filled with children, two cats and a dog constantly treading on the herbs, fragrance floats freely in the windows.

Every garden has its unique set of conditions and a gardener can learn much by observing and experimenting. Of course, no gardener is really in complete control and the occasional sunflower or *Nicotiana* will pop up between the stones, its seed dropped by a passing bird.

Here are three garden plans, all quite easy to get established.

A TEA GARDEN: If you are starting from seed, follow the directions on the seed packet

for proper spacing. If you are planting established plants, use six each of horehound, chamomile, lemon balm and dandelion; three each of spearmint and catnip. Caution: Use barriers made of metal strips to control the spreading of spearmint, and remove dandelion flowers before they go to seed, also to control spreading.

A SHELF GARDEN: If you are starting from seed, follow the directions on the seed packet for proper spacing. If you are planting established plants, use six of each kind. Many of the herbs in this design are easily direct sown in the garden: basil, chervil, chive, coriander, dill, fennel, sage and savory. Some of the perennial plants should be divided after two or three years.

Annuals, perennials and herbs—lavender, santolina, nasturtiums, roses and pansies—are combined in Rosalind Creasy's front entrance.

Creeping thyme, chamomile and marjoram growing between slate in this terrace garden show just how durable herbs can be.

GARDEN PLANS

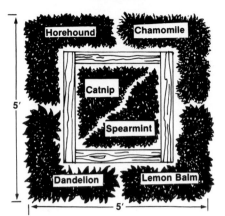

Tea Garden

Here's an easy little garden to keep you well-stocked with your favorite herbal teas!

Shelf Garden

Herbs grow happily in narrow areas that don't provide enough room for vegetables. This garden will fill your spice rack with the most popular herbal seasonings.

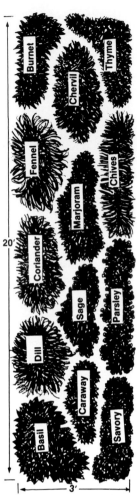

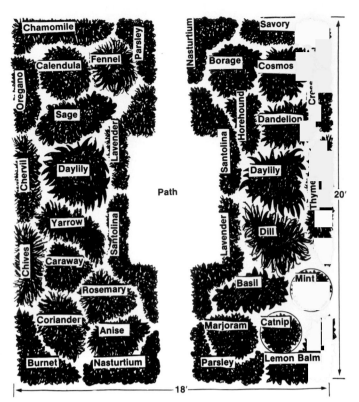

Herbs 'n Flowers Display Garden

The above garden plan illustrates attractive planting combinations of fragrant herbs along with flowers noted for their edible or dye qualities. Portions of this sample garden plan may be adapted for smaller gardens.

WINNING PLANT COMBINATIONS

Here are some handsome combinations you might try in your garden.

The blue-green of tricolored sage contrasts with the bright golden green foliage of silvery thyme.

Contrasting foliage of Stachys byzantina *(front) and* Stachys officinalis.

Scented geraniums, with different textures, colors and shapes, create a pleasing patchwork of foliage.

The silvery foliage and deep blue flowers of lavender contrast with the soft green foliage and pale yellow flowers of Santolina, *here in a carpet of creeping thyme.*

The striking blue, star-shaped flowers of borage complement the brilliant yellow of Calendula—*always a winning combination.*

Purple ruffled basil foliage is a strong contrast in color and shape with the light green, compact leaves of bush basil.

The use of 'Simplicity' shrub roses in the herb border gives interest of color when underplanted with lavender.

The furry gray leaves of Stachys *intertwine with a variegated nasturtium.*

Silver thyme is used to border a colorful ornamental vegetable garden.

HERBS 'N FLOWERS DIS-PLAY GARDEN: Many of the herbs in this plan are best sown directly into the garden; follow the proper spacing directions on the seed packets. If you are planting established plants, six of each kind will give a full, lush look. Some of the perennial plants should be divided after two or three years to avoid crowding.

HERBS IN CONTAINERS

Plants in pots require richer soil than those growing in your garden. Pro Mix or a similar commercial potting mix will work well. Provide proper drainage by making a hole in the bottom of the container. Herbs in pots tend to dry out quickly and will need a little more attention than those in the garden; try using cocoa hulls or mulch around the base of potted herbs to keep the plants from drying out too quickly. A weak solution of fish emulsion or other organic fertilizer monthly will keep your plants looking healthy. Tender herbs like bay, rosemary, lavender and lavender cotton are good potted herbs. They can be held over in a greenhouse during winter. Check in springtime to see if the roots are crowded, growing out of the bottom of the pots. If so, a larger pot is needed.

You don't need lots of room for potted herbs. Arrange some pots on the steps at your back door or fill a wooden barrel (or half barrel) with your favorites. Apartment dwellers can use window boxes (dark ruffled basil and pink petunias are lovely) and hanging baskets filled with parsley, thyme, winter savory, sweet marjoram or nasturtium. Simply tuck some of your favorite herbs in with any of your potted flowers. Herbs in containers are easy to move around to take better advantage of sunlight.

A silver herb garden in a pot.

A garden of herbs can be grown in containers.

Some herbs don't know their place. Herbs of the mint family, catnip and oregano, for example, tend to take over the garden. Planting in containers is one way to ensure the control of those overeager plants. You will also save the work of having to dig and pot your winter supply of indoor herbs. Try planting herbs in chimney flues which can be artfully arranged on a terrace—a neat and inexpensive way to display them.

A window box of culinary herbs: opal basil, sage, parsley and rosemary.

HERB COMBINATIONS FOR CONTAINERS

Assorted mints look great in pots on a patio or deck where they are readily available for use in iced tea and summer drinks.

Fill a strawberry pot with ingredients for a salad: lettuce, dill, chive and nasturtium. It will look pretty and provide the cook with fresh salad fixings.

Pasta sauce ingredients like oregano, basil and bay can all be tucked into a whiskey barrel and placed near the kitchen.

Create a home source of bouquets garnis by potting up parsley, thyme and bay, the three main ingredients.

Culinary herbs can be grown in a portable wooden tray.

FLOWERING HERBS IN A BARREL

Herb gardens are wonderfully practical because they are both useful and decorative. These aromatic herbs grown in a barrel are perfect for when you have just a little bit of extra space. You can find a half whiskey barrel at most garden supply stores; check to make sure that it has drainage holes. A circular bed can also be used if you want to expand the design. This garden will be especially welcome right outside the kitchen door so you can have fresh herbs in easy reach all summer long.

Flowering herbs in a barrel.

FLOWERING HERBS IN A BARREL

	Common Name	Scientific Name	Color	Height	Bloom	Number of Plants
A	Lavender	*Lavandula*	Lavender with blue, gray	2½ feet	June–July	4
B	Borage	*Borago*	Blue	1½ feet	June–August	4
C	Catnip	*Nepeta cataria*	Purple	1½ feet	July–September	4
D	Chives	*Allium schoenoprasum*	Purple	2 feet	June	6
E	Sage	*Salvia officinalis*	Silver with green	1–2 feet	June	6

When planting from seed: Use 1 seed packet for each variety.

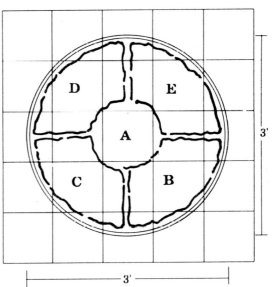

THE HERB PLANTING AND GROWING GUIDE

SOIL PREPARATION

The first step in preparing your herb garden is choosing a good spot, strategically located for best enjoyment. To ensure success with herbs, as with all plants, you need good drainage. Most herbs also appreciate lots of sun and some protection from cold winter winds. Because many herbs are perennials that will live and perform in one place for years, prepare the soil well. A bit of hard work now will mean less work later and help avoid disappointment. Herbs are not fussy plants, but they appreciate a well-prepared home. If the location is right, drainage is good and the soil is loose and free of weeds, your plants will flourish. Herbs are very tolerant plants; they thrive in less-than-perfect soil conditions. In most cases, in fact, soil that is too rich will inhibit their production of essential oils and diminish their fragrance and flavor.

Mark the desired shape and size of your new garden bed and begin the process of removing any lawn or brush growing on the site. Next, spade the soil to the depth of 18 inches. The upper portion of soil, the dark topsoil, is where you will find the most nutrients; when you fill the hole back in, you want to put this topsoil down where the plants' roots will come in contact with its valuable nutrients. Start layering in your 18-inch hole, beginning with a layer of compost, then peat moss, lime and well-rotted manure. Spade all these ingredients well and rake the area level. If you are preparing the site in spring allow several weeks before planting for the mixture to settle.

A perfect time to prepare the soil for a successful growing season is in fall, after the harvest and before the first frost. A fall tillage will make spring preparation easier. It will also give the compost and any lime that you add time to work thoroughly into the soil. A soil test is worth the modest investment if the gardener is preparing a new bed. Your local County Extension service will examine your soil samples and assess the soil's texture and fertilizer requirements, and whether the pH should be adjusted by the addition of lime. (Lime takes months to break down into a form usable by the plants.) If site preparation has been done in fall, the soil will have plenty of time to settle. When you prepare in advance, you need only add a bit of slow-release fertilizer—some well-rotted manure or compost—in spring, and once again turn the soil over to loosen it for the new seedlings or seed you wish to plant.

Drainage is the most important part of soil preparation. Without proper drainage, all of your hard work is futile. Poor drainage means poor root development and roots sitting in water, and drowned roots deprived of air will mean stunted growth and certain disaster. To check for proper drainage, dig a hole 1 foot deep. Fill the hole with water and allow the water to settle overnight. If the hole is full of the water in the morning you have a serious drainage problem.

One cause of poor drainage is a soil that is heavy in clay. A simple test can be done to determine the type of soil you have. Squeeze a handful of wet soil. If it holds together, you

Silver and green Santolina *are used to edge an herb garden.*

Clay soil

Sandy soil

Loamy soil

have clay. If it falls through your fingers, you have sandy soil. If it shows the imprint of your fingers and then slowly crumbles as you release it, your soil has the right texture for successful gardening. Both clay and sandy soils can be amended by adding organic matter, compost or peat moss. A raised bed may be the answer to a drainage problem.

RAISED BEDS

There are many advantages to growing your herbs in raised beds. Raised beds are an excellent way to provide the necessary drainage. The soil will also warm up sooner in spring and you can plant as much as two weeks before the soil in an open garden is ready for planting. It becomes easier within the confines of a raised bed to organize your herbs and to keep the entire bed looking neat. If the beds are no wider than 4 feet you can easily work from either side without stepping into the garden; that way you never have a problem with soil compaction, a problem that impedes good growth. The wooden frames of the raised beds also make comfortable spots to sit while you weed and tend your garden.

Raised beds shaped in rectangles aren't difficult to build. Outline the rectangular bed with pressure-treated boards (they last in the garden for 10 or more years), 2-by-6s or 2-by-8s. Set them in the ground in a 2-inch-deep ditch. Leave a path around and between the beds and shovel the topsoil from the paths into the beds. Add compost, well-rotted manure and any additional topsoil until the mixture is level with the top of the boards. In time it will settle just below the top of the boards. Fill the paths with shredded bark or wood chips.

Testing the Soil

Fall is the best time to take a soil test, a test that will tell you exactly what you need to add to your soil to prepare it for a good growing season. A soil test will give you a reading of the acidity or alkalinity of your soil. This is a pH reading, on a scale from 0 to 14 where 7 is neutral. Herbs prefer a slightly acid soil, so consider anything between 6 and 7 (even to 7.5) acceptable. A soil test is easy; instructions are included with every commercial soil kit, available in garden stores or through garden catalogs. You can also send a soil sample to your local Agriculture Extension Service. They will send you a reading together with complete instructions on what is needed to bring your soil to the ideal state for growing herbs. Most soils in the eastern United States already are slightly acid, which will allow you to grow many of the plants you wish, including nearly all the herbs. However, yearly additions of compost and such mulches as pine needles will cause some fluctuation in acidity.

COMPOST AND COMPOSTING

Composting is the word of the century. Training people to compost could help solve our difficult garbage problems and enrich our earth. Compost, or "black gold," as it is lovingly called by some gardeners, is a well-balanced meal for your plants. Using compost to enrich your herb garden is much safer than using chemical fertilizers, which sometimes actually rob herbs of their fragrant oils. Composting is a year-'round task and a constantly rewarding one.

Creating a compost pile is as easy as choosing an out-of-the-way spot to deposit all leaves, grass clippings and other biodegradable materials. Simply add to the pile and allow it to break down over time. A finished compost pile produces dark, nutritious humus that will improve the texture of your garden soil. Leaving the job to nature, it takes at least six months to decompose. Look around you and you will find many useful ingredients to add to your compost pile. Kitchen waste, including vegetable peels, eggshells and rotten fruit, makes wonderful compost. And nothing is better than autumn leaves (with the exception of black walnut). Add them to your compost, keep them moist and turn the pile occasionally. If you want the compost ready sooner, chop the leaves up to give their surface more exposure to the microbes in the pile that do the work of composting. A lawn mower or leaf shredder can do the shredding for you. When you run out of good fall leaves to compost, ask your neighbors for their plastic bags full of fall leaves. These leaves belong in a compost pile and not in the local landfill.

Compost Bin Design

Most gardeners find it neater to contain their compost pile. Your compost container can be as simple as a circle of wire mesh, about 4 feet high, wrapped around four solid stakes set in the ground deep enough to provide permanent support. Or you can set concrete blocks as three sides of a rectangle, leaving the fourth side open to allow you access to the finished compost. Finally, plastic compost bins are available from garden catalogs and garden stores; they do an excellent job and look neat in a corner of the garden.

Speeding up the Compost

Some gardeners recommend that you layer the compost ingredients to speed up the process. Dead leaves, grass clippings that have not been treated with weed killer, weeds that have not gone to seed and vegetable matter such as peelings of fruit and vegetables (especially when cut into small pieces) make excellent compost, as do tea leaves and coffee grounds and the remains of salads. I keep two bags for garbage. Into one I put meat, fish and greasy leavings that would attract animals; this is the bag I put out for municipal collection. In the other bag I keep anything that makes good mulch, and this goes nightly onto the compost pile.

Start your compost pile on a layer of twigs or small branches or on cinder blocks, to allow good air circulation. When you achieve about a 6-inch layer of compost, dust the top with lime and add an inch of garden soil. Repeat these layers and keep the pile moist. The top, if made concave (by shallowly digging out the center of the pile) provides a catch basin for rain water, which brings its own ingredients to further improve the pile. The pile needs to be moist but not soaked. You mustn't drown the bacteria that decompose for you, and while they work they heat the pile. Every so often, turn the pile so the material around the edges gets to the inside area where the work of breaking down the ingredients into good loam takes place. With this method, you'll make compost faster and have more good loam for your garden. Still, even left alone, time and compost material with help from the bacteria in it, work well all by themselves. The method you use for composting depends on how much of a hurry you are in for your finished product. Bear in mind that there's never enough good compost.

What to put in the compost pile:
Remember that the smaller that the pieces are, the faster they will decompose:

Shredded or whole fall leaves (first drag a lawn mower back and forth over leaves to shred, or use a leaf shredder)
Shredded bark (you'll need a wood chipper for this)
Shredded twigs
Fresh vegetable and fruit peelings
Grass cuttings (not treated with herbicides)
Tea leaves
Coffee grounds
Well-rotted horse or cow manure
Eggshells
Cut flowers
Pine needles

What not to put in the compost pile:

Cooked food
Weeds with seedpods
Raw fish and animal remains (good compost, but they attract mice and other small animals)
Diseased plants (the disease will spread)
Any plant material that has been treated with herbicide or pesticide within the past three weeks

This compost starter bin is easy to make from four 4-foot posts, set in a square or rectangle, wrapped in chicken wire. If the chicken wire is secured loosely on the fourth side, the bin can be opened easily for removal of compost or for working the compost pile.

PLANTING

Transplant your herb plants on an overcast day or in late afternoon, to protect them from exposure to strong sun. Space the plants as indicated in "Plant Portraits." Firm soil well around the stems, leaving a shallow depression around each to hold water. Water well. If you are worried about cold evening temperatures, place a garden blanket or Hot Kap over plants for several nights as added protection. The first few weeks are critical for healthy root development. Don't allow new plants to dry out too much between watering. However, once herbs are well established, many of them tolerate dry spells, even drought.

Soil Readiness for Spring Planting

By preparing your garden in autumn, the soil is ready too, and all that hard work in fall will finally pay off. Avoid working soil that is quite wet because the soil structure can be damaged. If you till soil when it is too wet, it will ruin the granular structure. The soil will compress and resist the tender roots that try to grow there. It could take an entire season to recover its natural consistency or be damaged permanently. The best test to judge when the soil is ready to work is the one that farmers used hundreds of years ago (and still use today). Pick up a fistful of soil. If it sticks together in a ball, it is too wet to work; if it readily breaks apart, it is dry enough to begin your spring soil preparation.

HERBS THAT GROW IN PARTIAL SHADE

Aconite
Angelica
Balm (lemon)
Borage
Burnet
Chervil
Comfrey
Costmary
Fennel
Foxglove
Germander
Mint
Parsley
Pennyroyal (American and
    English)
Perilla
Rosemary
Sage (all kinds)
Santolina (gray)
Sweet woodruff
Tarragon (French)
Thyme (all kinds)
Violet (common)
Winter savory
Wormwood (all kinds)

HERBS THAT GROW IN MOIST AREAS

Angelica
Lovage
Mint
Monarda
Parsley
Pennyroyal (English)
Violet (common)

A lush herb garden at Mohonk Mountain House.

HERBS FOR GROUNDCOVER

Chamomile (Roman)
Sweet woodruff
Thyme (caraway and lemon)
Violet (common)
Wormwood

HERBS WITH SHOWY FLOWERS

Calendula
Chive
Fennel
Feverfew
Foxglove
Geranium
Germander
Hyssop
Lavender

Monarda
Nasturtium
Rose
Rosemary
Rue
Salvia
Tansy
Violet

MULCHES

Next to compost, mulch is a gardener's best friend. It helps conserve moisture in the soil, it smothers unwanted weeds and, most important, keeps the soil temperature uniform. It also warms the early spring soil. During hot, late-summer days it cools the roots of your plants. As some mulches break down over the season they add important nutrients to the soil. Avoid using grass as mulch because it takes nutrients from the soil as it breaks down. Beware: Slugs like to hide beneath the cool layer of mulch. Mulches may be pine needles, straw, shredded leaves, cocoa shells and buckwheat hulls.

PROPAGATION

Division

The best way to propagate many of the perennial herbs is through root division. This is a gardener's bonus. Perennials may take two seasons to get truly established, but after three years or so, you can divide and share your bounty with the neighborhood. Division is not only a great way to acquire more plants, it is also beneficial to the plants. It gives them the space they need to flourish.

The method of dividing depends on the particular herb. Usually a sharp, clean knife is the best tool. Be careful to provide each divided portion with enough root for successful growth. Replant immediately whenever possible. If it isn't possible, keep the roots damp, wrapped in wet newspaper until you can replant. The best time to divide herbs is usually in autumn or early spring. Autumn is my choice because the weather is cool and less stressful to the "new" plants. Replanted in fall, the herbs have all winter through early spring to bounce back. Some herbs best propagated by root division are yarrow, chive, costmary and purple coneflower.

Propagation from Stem Cuttings

Perennials are slow to grow from seed, waiting until their second or sometimes third season to flourish. To speed up the process you can take stem cuttings. Many herbs, the scented geraniums, for example, are easy to propagate this way.

To grow from cuttings: Cut a 3- to 4-inch piece of a stem that is new growth, not old (tough) or too new (weak). To avoid damaging the stem tissue, use a sharp, clean knife. Make the cut ½ inch below a node (the place a leaf is attached to the stem), or at the point a pair of leaves come together at the stem; this ensures the cutting will have sufficient energy to sustain it until it can produce roots.

Limit the number of leaves on the cutting to two; more leaves, or buds, will cause stress; more leaves will cause wilting, and drain the stem of much-needed energy required to

Make a cut about ½ inch below a node.

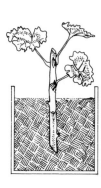

Gently firm the rooting medium around the stem.

A clear plastic covering ensures a moister environment for the cutting.

produce roots. The stem should be kept moist. Keep it wrapped in wet newspaper or in water until you can plant it. (Plastic bags and wet paper towels are standard supplies of traveling gardeners.) Fill a pot with moist, not soggy, rooting medium. You can make your own rooting medium by mixing sterile sand and vermiculite, or purchase a ready-made mix. Dip the node end of the stem in a rooting hormone (available in garden supply stores —look for one that contains a fungicide). It is best to shake a small amount of rooting hormone onto a paper towel and dip the stem into it, then discard the remaining hormone. Don't just dip the cutting into the jar of hormone powder; this can spread fungus, the main cause of root propagation failure. Next, make a 1-inch hole with a clean pencil or stick into the rooting medium. Stand the stem in the hole, node end first, and gently press the moistened medium around the stem. Roots will then grow out of the node.

Cover the pot with a plastic bag, making sure that the plastic does not touch the cutting's leaves. It is helpful to place a wooden ice-cream stick on either side of the cutting to support the bag. Close the bag with a twist tie to ensure a moist atmosphere for root development. Place the pot in a warm location (70° to 80° F). The two main ingredients for successful root development are moisture and warmth. If you are concerned that too much moisture has developed inside the bag, simply allow some air to circulate by releasing the tie (a musty odor and mildew visible on the soil indicate conditions that are too moist). Reclose the bag after a day. Keep pots away from direct sunlight until the roots develop.

Plants develop roots at different rates, so be patient and keep your stem cuttings moist and warm. Once roots have developed, remove the pot from the bag and place the cutting in light. To see if roots have developed, gently pull on the cutting. Any resistance will mean that the process has started. This takes about a month. If the stem turns black, remove it.

Propagation by Layering

Layering is the easiest form of propagating. Layering allows the plants to do the work, with just a little help from you. Rosemary and sweet marjoram are two good layering candidates.

Other plants that also work well are low-growing herbs that tend to send out roots as they run around the garden. To propagate by layering, follow these simple rules:

1. Remove a few inches of leaves from the lower-growing stems.
2. Bend the leafy ends to create an arch.
3. Pile some growing medium over the stripped portion.
4. Hold the stripped portion in place with a large hairpin, clothespin, bent wire or even a stone.
5. Water the area thoroughly where the stripped portion touches the medium.
6. Check the stripped portion after about four weeks. If the roots have connected, cut the new plant from the parent plant. Dig it up and replant it or pot it.

Herbal Helpers

Many gardeners plant "helpers" near vegetables and flowers to combat insects, stimulate growth and intensify flavor. These helper herbs are believed to have characteristics that make them ideal companions to certain other plants in the garden. Some flowering herbs (borage, lavender, sage, savory, thyme) are good neighbors for all plants because they attract bees. By contrast, some herbs are detrimental to certain crops because they attract insects or diseases to which the crops are sensitive. Aromatic herbs add vigor to cabbage and kale, but should not be planted near cucumbers. Don't plant fennel near beans or tomatoes.

Below are listed some of the most popular herbs, and the plants they seem to help (and a few it is believed they hurt), as well as the beneficial effects. (Please note: These recommendations come from gardeners' experiences, not from scientific tests.)

Herb	Companion Crops	Effects of Herb
Basil	Asparagus, lettuce, tomato	Enhances flavor and growth, repels flies
Borage	Squash, strawberry, tomato	Repels tomato worm
Chamomile	Cabbage, onion	Enhances flavor and growth
Chervil	Radish	Enhances flavor and growth
Chive	Carrot, tomato	Chases aphids
Coriander	Anise	Enhances growth
Dill	Cabbage, cucumber; don't plant with carrots, onions, lettuce	Enhances flavor and growth
Garlic	Parsnip, lettuce, raspberry, rose	Repels aphids and Japanese beetles, enhances flavor
Mint	Cabbage, tomato	Repels white cabbage moth, enhances flavor
Oregano	Bean	Enhances growth
Parsley	Asparagus, corn, tomato	Repels asparagus beetle, enhances flavor and growth
Rosemary	Bean, cabbage, carrot	Repels carrot fly, cabbage moth and bean beetles
Sage	Cabbage, carrot; don't plant with cucumber	Repels carrot fly and cabbage moth
Summer savory	Bean	Repels bean beetles, enhances growth

BRING YOUR HERBS INDOORS

For indoor enjoyment in late summer, pot up some herbs, but be careful not to disturb the roots. Water the pots generously and set the plants in a shady outdoor place for a week. Before bringing them inside check for insects. In order for the herbs to make sufficient leaf growth during the winter, plants must have plenty of sunlight and a temperature maintained well above freezing at all times. Don't expect them to grow to the same size they would in an outdoor garden, but they will grow well and lush and provide you with fresh herbs that beat the flavor of dried or frozen herbs. Herbs, while very tolerant in the garden, are less tolerant than most houseplants. They need perfect conditions. Here are some rules to observe when growing herbs indoors:

LIGHT: Most herbs indoors must have at least five hours of direct sunlight a day. The exceptions are mint, bay, parsley, rosemary, thyme and myrtle, which prefer partial shade. Natural sunlight can be supplemented or replaced with fluorescent light. A two-tube, cool white fixture hung 6 to 8 inches above the plants and left on for 14 to 16 hours a day will keep herb plants healthy, happy and productive. Plants on the windowsill must be turned regularly. This keeps them shapely, making sure all sides of the plants receive sufficient light.

TEMPERATURE: Grow herb plants in cooler temperatures. A daytime temperature of 65°F and nighttime temperature of 55° to 60°F are best. Make sure all plants are moved away from windowpanes, especially during freezing weather.

SOIL: Potted herbs appreciate a relatively rich soil mixture with good drainage. Use a good commercial potting mixture and provide a large enough pot for good root development.

FERTILIZATION: Care must be taken to give your plants enough food to keep them productive but not so much they lose their fragrant oils. A feeding once a month with seaweed or fish emulsion at about half-strength makes a good herb food. Both of these natural fertilizers are available from your local nursery.

WATER: When to water and how much to water are tricky questions to answer. It is important to water herbs regularly, but they can be finicky. Water most herbs thoroughly when the soil surface starts to dry out. Always use room-temperature water. Never allow soils to become waterlogged or pots to sit in water. These conditions bring on root rot and other fungal diseases. It is for this reason we stress the importance of a well-drained potting mixture.

Potted herbs wintering over on a sunny windowsill.

AIR CIRCULATION: Herbs are sensitive to dry, stagnant air, which promotes fungal diseases and insect infestation. On the other hand, a constant draft is deadly to herbs. Try to keep the air moving around the plants by opening a window slightly in an adjoining room or using a fan (not directly pointed at the plants) for better cross-ventilation. Be sure to give plants plenty of space so air can circulate around and between them. Don't crowd plants or let the foliage from one plant touch the neighboring plant. If the air is very dry, set the pots on a pebble-lined tray filled with an inch or less of water, making sure the pots are resting on the pebbles and not sitting in water. This will add humidity to the air around them.

HERBS FOR GROWING INDOORS

Balm (lemon)
Basil (dwarf green and
    dark opal)
Chervil
Chive
Dill (fern leaf)
Mint
Oregano
Parsley
Rosemary
Sage
Scented geranium
Summer savory
Sweet marjoram
Tarragon
Thyme

PLANT PORTRAITS

More than 65 herbs are described in the following pages. Some are perennial, others annual or biennial. In the case of perennials we list the hardiness zones in which they will thrive. In the case of annuals, zones are not important because these are plants that can be grown successfully in every region of the country. Each herb has its own set of wonderful attributes. Some are fragrant, others edible and still others make attractive ornamental additions to the garden. Select some of the mentioned plants for your herb garden, and try others in your flower borders or potted on a deck or terrace. Delight in their beauty and durability.

The plants are listed under their botanical (Latin) names and cross-referenced by their common names. This is to help you avoid confusion. Every known plant has a first name, the genus (indicated by the first Latin word), a grouping of plants with similar characteristics. Every plant also has a second name, the species (the second Latin word), and this identifies shared qualities of lesser importance. Although common names are easier to pronounce, they can lead to misunderstandings because many different plants grown in different parts of the country have the same common name. Using botanical names is the one way to be sure of having the correct cultural information. We hope that these plant portraits will give a better understanding of herbs and how to grow them successfully.

PLANT PORTRAIT KEY

Here is a guide to the symbols and terms we use throughout this section.

Latin name of the herb is in boldface italic.

Phonetic pronunciation of the Latin name is in parentheses.

Common name of the herb is in boldface type.

The average hours of sun needed per day is indicated by symbols. The first symbol is what the plant prefers, but the plant is adaptable to all conditions lists.

○ *Sun*—Six hours or longer of direct sunlight per day.
◑ *Part shade*—Three to six hours of direct sunlight per day.
● *Shade*—Two hours or less of direct sunlight per day.

Symbols for:
◆ *Drought resistant*
✹ *Heat lover*
✳ *Cool-weather plant*
🕯 *Long-lasting cut flower*
🍴 *Edible/culinary herb*
❀ *Fragrant blooms or foliage*
🌿 *Suitable for drying*
♨ *Tolerates moist soil*

Grade of Difficulty: Plants that take the least amount of care are identified as "easy."

Digitalis, *now used as an ornamental flower, was once grown as a medicinal herb.*

These plants are good choices for beginning gardeners with little time.

Heights are for normal growth, but plants with very fertile soil and a longer growing season may grow taller. Conversely, with poor growing conditions, the plant could be shorter.

Native American are those plants that were growing on the American continent when the pilgrims arrived. Most herbs, however, were brought here from Mediterranean climates.

Zones: Check The USDA Plant Hardiness Map (pages 92–93), based on average annual temperatures for each area—or zone—of the United States to see what zone you live in. The plant portrait lists the zones best for that plant; in the case of annuals, however, no zone is given because the plant will grow virtually anywhere.

Cultural Information: Plants' preferences and information how best to grow your plants are given here. We recommend the easiest and best methods of increasing your number of plants. Some plants are best grown from seed, others from division, and so on.

Achillea filipendula
'Gold Plate'

Alchemilla *species*

Achillea (a-KIL-lee-a) **yarrow**, Native American, easy, perennial. ○ ◗ ✳ 🐞 🌿
Zones: 3 to 8
Height: 1½ to 2 feet
Characteristics: Yarrow (*Achillea Millefolium*) is a long blooming and rugged perennial herb. It will quickly establish handsome colonies in the border. The

yellow yarrow flowers bloom from June through September and make wonderful cut flowers for fresh or dried arrangements. Yarrow leaves are deeply cut, fernlike and gray-green in color with a pungent fragrance when touched or stripped from the stems. Yarrow was once used by Native Americans as a medicinal herb. It was applied to open wounds, to help control bleeding and cause the blood to clot faster. Yarrow is native to Europe and naturalized in most of North America. Try 'Red Beauty' and 'Fern Leaf'.
Cultural Information: Plant yarrow 2½ to 3 feet apart, in well-drained soil in fall or late spring after all danger of frost is past. Cut the plant back to a few inches from the ground after flowering to help induce bushiness and increase blooms. For rejuvenation, divide every three to four years in early spring or late fall. To avoid stem rot, water the plant early in the day, especially in moist climates. Yarrow prefers soils that are not especially fertile, so avoid excessive use of nitrogen fertilizers. Although this plant is considered drought resistant, it does appreciate a good watering during dry, hot weather. After the plants are several inches high, mulch the soil between them with compost or other material that will decompose in one season to add nutrients to the soil, keep weeds down and to conserve moisture. Yarrow is generally pest-free due to its pungent foliage and is easily grown from seed. Yarrow is credited with attracting beneficial insects, including lady beetles. Germination takes from 10 to 14 days;

the optimum temperature is 65° to 70°F.
Uses: Ornamental herb, can be used in both fresh and dried arrangements. Aromatic herb, can be used as an insect repellent.

Alchemilla (al-kem-ILL-a) **lady's-mantle**, easy, perennial. ◐ ○ ✳ 🌿
Zones: 3 to 8
Height: 6 to 12 inches
Characteristics: Lady's-mantle (*Alchemilla vulgaris*) is a low-growing, graceful perennial with large, pleated, silvery green leaves. The leaves have tiny hairs that collect rain and dew, which form little silvery beads that glisten in a gemlike fashion. The dew collected from leaves was once thought to have medicinal powers. As an added bonus, small clusters of fragrant, yellow-green flowers bloom in late spring. Today lady's-mantle is grown for its graceful, ornamental beauty. It grows from 6 to 12 inches tall and is valued as a lovely groundcover. Try planting it as a border edging and allow it to spill over onto paths and walkways. Try planting lady's-mantle in front of Jacob's ladder (*Polemonium caeruleum*), an attractive, early-blooming, blue perennial. The striking blue of Jacob's ladder makes a handsome combination with the yellow flowers of lady's-mantle.
Cultural Information: Lady's-mantle thrives in cool weather, part shade and well-drained soil. Sow seeds in a cold frame in early spring. After danger of frost place the plants 4 to 6 inches apart in the garden. If the flower heads are allowed to go to seed, they will self-sow,

creating a crop of tiny plants in early spring. These seedlings can be either left or moved to new locations.

Harvest: Cut the flowers for winter bouquets at the peak of bloom and hang them upside down in a drying room.

Uses: Ornamental herb, dried or fresh flowers can be used in arrangements.

Allium sativum (AL-lee-um) **garlic**, easy, perennial. ○ ◑ ⫙ ⅏

Zones: 3 to 10 (grow as an annual in Zone 10)

Height: 4 feet

Characteristics: Garlic is both useful and ornamental. Garlic flowers are showy clusters of pink and whitish globes, which bloom from June to July amid flat, dark green, grasslike foliage. The flowers look lovely in arrangements and the petals can be tossed in salads. After flowering cut back stalks if you want cloves. Usually found in herb and vegetable gardens, it is a strong-smelling, bulbous plant. The bulb consists of 8 to 10 distinct segments, or cloves. Garlic was once believed to possess spiritual powers and used to drive away evil spirits; today it is mostly grown for use in cooking. It is a native of the Mediterranean. Garlic is a useful companion plant for rose, cabbage, eggplant, tomato, and fruit trees, to help control insects. Medicinally, garlic was once thought to control a range of ailments from high blood pressure to stomach disorders. Today the Chinese claim great success with treating stomach disorders using garlic, but scientific research has not confirmed this claim.

Cultural Information: Plant garlic cloves in fall or early spring in a sunny, well-drained spot. Place cloves 2 inches deep into the loose earth 4 to 6 inches apart and cover the area with well-rotted cow manure and a sprinkling of bone meal. Space the rows 12 inches apart. Thin, grasslike blades will emerge and continue to grow into fall. If you live in an area where thawing and freezing occur, mulch with salt hay to prevent heaving. In spring the growing process will resume. Keep the garden weeded and watered during dry spells. Because of its strong odor insects are rarely a problem.

Harvest: In late August after the leaves have yellowed, the bulbs can be lifted and cured in an airy, dry spot for 2 to 3 weeks or so. Discard any rotted bulbs. Remember to clean off the dry, loose soil before storing the garlic in open containers, such as baskets. Garlic can be stored all winter for use in cooking (if properly cured).

Uses: Culinary herb, can be used in butter, cheese, breads, stuffings, sauces, salad dressings, soups, fish and vinegar. A spray of garlic juice and water will keep aphids in control.

Allium Schoenoprasum (AL-lee-um) **chive**, easy, perennial. ○ ◑ ⫙ ⅏

Zones: 3 to 10

Height: 1 to 1½ feet

Characteristics: Chive is an undemanding herb that adds interest to any garden. It forms dark green clumps of tubular, grasslike leaves. Chive flowers are fluffy lavender pompoms that bloom in late spring. Chive's

Allium sativum

Allium Schoenoprasi

leaves have a mild onion flavor. Both the flowers and foliage of chive are edible.

Cultural Information: Chive will thrive in rich, well-worked, moist soil but is not fussy and adjusts to most soil types. A topdressing of well-rotted manure or compost added annually is all the fertilizer needed. The chive seed germinates somewhat slowly and requires darkness. It is easier and quicker to propagate by dividing clumps every few years. Chive is a good companion plant for carrot, grape and rose because its strong odor rids plants of aphids. Used as a border around your rose garden, chive is both attractive and helpful as its pungent odor deters Japanese beetles and other insects that spread black spot. If your plant looks haggard in midsummer or if the shoots diminish, snip the mature plants to within 2 inches of the ground, water heavily and scratch in some compost or organic fertilizer. Chive multiplies quickly, so it is best to divide it every third year. Because it needs a cold rest period to retain its vigor, is best to sow seeds in pots for indoor winter use.

Aloysia triphylla

Harvest: Harvest chive any time by simply cutting the slender, tubular leaves as needed. After the flower stalks have blossomed, cut them off close to the ground.

Uses: Culinary herb, leaves can be used in salads, potatoes and soups; can be used to flavor vinegar. It is an excellent potted plant.

Aloysia (a-LOY-see-a) **lemon verbena**, moderate, shrub.

Zones: 9 to 10
Height: 3 to 5 feet
Characteristics: Lemon verbena (*Aloysia*, sometimes called *Lippia citriodora*) is a deciduous woody shrub with a lovely lemony fragrance and attractive, light green leaves, pointed and fringed with hairs. The tiny lavender flowers of lemon verbena bloom in late summer and fall. It is a native to Chile and Argentina.
Cultural Information: Plant lemon verbena in rich, moist soil in full sun. Lemon verbena can be propagated by cuttings taken in late summer. In especially warm climates it can reach more than 10 to 15 feet in height. North of Zone 9 it is best grown as a container plant and

Anethum graveolens

protected from winter weather. Remember when bringing indoors for winter that the leaves will drop, because it is a deciduous shrub.
Harvest: The leaves of lemon verbena can be cut at any time. Cut plant back in midsummer to keep its full, compact shape.
Uses: Culinary herb, can be used to flavor cold beverages and teas.

Anethum graveolens (an-E-thum) **dill**, easy, annual.

Height: 3 feet
Characteristics: Dill graces your garden with feathery foliage and lovely pale yellow, umbrella-shaped flowers. Try using this attractive herb in both your vegetable and your flower gardens. It has long wisps of leaves that are bluish green, with feathery tips, like fennel. Dill stands about 3 feet high and should be planted toward the back of the garden border. In this position it can provide a wonderful backdrop that helps display shorter plants. Dill is also a useful companion plant that will enhance the growth of onion, lettuce and cabbage. It is native to southern Europe. A new variety, 'Dwarf Fernleaf', is compact and doesn't go to seed very quickly.
Cultural Information: Dill is a heavy feeder and requires rich, well-drained soil. Prepare the soil in early spring with compost and well-rotted cow manure. Dill does not like to be transplanted so it is best to direct sow into the garden. Thin to 10 inches apart when the plants are 2 inches tall. For a continuous supply plant seed every three weeks throughout the growing season. Choose its garden spot carefully as dill tends

to reseed, returning year after year. Germination will take 10 to 21 days, at temperatures of 65°F. Remember to keep the soil moist until the seed germinates and has established a good root system.
Harvest: Harvest fruiting umbels (flower clusters) when fully developed but not brown. Cut whole spray stem and tie in small bundles immediately. Hang in a dry, warm, airy place out of sun, to retain color. Seeds can be easily stripped by rubbing umbels between the palms of your hands. Fruiting tops can be used fresh or dried. Dill loses some flavor when dried.
Uses: Culinary herb, dried seeds (ground or whole) can be used in soups, stews, sauces, fish, eggs, pickles, salads and vegetables. Ornamental herb, dried or fresh flower can be used in arrangements.

Angelica Archangelica (an-JELL-ik-a) **angelica**, easy, short lived perennial/biennial.

Zones: 3 to 6
Height: 4 to 8 feet
Characteristics: Grow angelica, a tropical-looking herb, for its fragrance, flavor and stately beauty. It is a decorative herb with a celerylike foliage and a pleasantly fragrant aroma that makes a wonderful addition to any garden border. This tall beauty should be planted at the back of a garden where it can reach remarkable heights, up to 8 feet, to tower over your garden. Every feature of angelica is dramatic, from its luxuriant divided leaves to its greenish yellow, 6-inch, globe-shaped flowers. Angelica is highly attractive

to bees. It is a native of northern Europe where it has been a favorite herb of poets and kings throughout history—it was used to drive away evil spirits, spells and enchantments. Today it is usually grown as a decorative feature at the back of the garden.

Cultural Information: Angelica doesn't fit neatly into any of the normal plant categories. Treated as a biennial, it is best propagated by seed in late summer. It will reach 2 to 3 feet in the first season but not flower until the second or third season. Angelica prefers a cool, shady spot with rich, moist, well-drained soil. Plant the seeds as soon as they ripen, because they are short lived. The seeds of angelica will germinate in four weeks at temperatures of 60°F. Seeds need light to germinate, so just press them gently into the soil, but don't cover. They also require cool, moist conditions. If you want to ensure the yearly return of angelica, allow it to flower and go to seed, so that it will self-sow and return to your garden year after year. Thin the plants in spring to stand 3 feet apart. Angelica can also be propagated through division but this tends to be more risky than seed propagation. Few disease and pest problems affect it, but remember to check for crown rot during very wet seasons.

Harvest: Harvest roots in fall of the first year, stems and leaves in spring of the second growing year. The seeds can be harvested as soon as they ripen.

Uses: Culinary herb, stems can be boiled like rhubarb or crystallized to use as a garnish. Fresh leaves can be used to flavor wines,

added to green salads, fruit soups and stews or used as a garnish. Aromatic herb, dried roots can be used in sachets and potpourri; seeds can be burned as incense.

Anise; see *Pimpinella*

Anthemis nobilis (AN-them-is) **Roman chamomile,** easy, perennial. ○ ◗ ⑪

Zones: 3 to 10
Height: 12 to 14 inches
Characteristics: The common name chamomile is used for two different plants, both easy to grow. Roman chamomile is a perennial and German chamomile (*Matricaria recutita*) is an annual. Both chamomiles are similar with feathery foliage, daisylike blossoms and apple flavor and fragrance. Believed to have many healing properties, chamomile was often planted alongside an ailing plant, to help speed recovery. Because of this trait it was lovingly called the "plants' physician." Gardeners believed that chamomile would bring health to any garden in which it was planted. Both types are native to Africa, Asia and Europe and have been naturalized in North America. Roman chamomile (*A. nobilis*) is a low-growing, extremely hardy herb. Because of its low-spreading habit, only 12 to 14 inches in height, it is often used as an attractive groundcover or flowering lawn. Roman chamomile has been used in walkways and paths since the Middle Ages; its pleasant scent is released when walked on. It has pretty flowers, yellow centers with single white florets, that bloom from May to August.

Angelica Archangelica

Cultural Information: Roman chamomile will grow in all types of soil provided it has good drainage. It thrives in moist soil and full sun. However, it is slow and difficult to germinate from seed. Seeds can be sown in early spring in a carefully prepared bed, but it is quicker and easier to propagate by offshoots or sets, which are produced by the mother plant. Space the plants 6 inches apart. Roman chamomile spreads easily and crowds out weeds. If used as a lawn, shear back during growing season to keep it attractive.

Harvest: When petals begin to turn back on the disk, collect the flowers and let dry completely.

Uses: Culinary herb, can be used as a tea. Can also be used as a hair rinse, to bring out golden highlights.

Anthemis nobilis

Anthriscus Cerefolium (an-THRIS-kus) **chervil, French parsley,** moderate, annual. ● ◑ ⑪

Height: 2 feet
Characteristics: Chervil has a delicate, aromatic scent and soft, pale green, lacy leaves with small white flowers that bloom

Anthriscus *species*

in May or June. It is attractive in any flower garden border. Chervil is sometimes called "gourmet parsley" because of its parsleylike flavor and appearance. The two main varieties of chervil are plain and curly. Chervil is native to Europe and Asia and has naturalized in North America.

Cultural Information: Chervil likes a moist, moderately rich soil that is well drained. Keep the flower clusters cut off to encourage branching. Chervil doesn't like transplanting and prefers to be sown directly in

Armoracia rusticana

Artemisia Absinthium

the garden where it is to grow. Be sure to keep the seeds moist for 7 to 28 days at 70°F until germination takes place. Because chervil tends to go to seed quickly, it is necessary to make several plantings from April until mid-July to ensure a continuous supply. When planted near radishes, chervil enhances their growth and flavor.

Harvest: Chervil is best used fresh. Cut the leaves as desired. It makes an attractive garnish. The leaves can be cooked like spinach and the roots can be boiled and eaten like potato. Dry the leaves on trays away from the sun to prevent discoloration. Store them in tightly covered containers. You can also freeze chervil, which helps preserve the flavor. Mix in a blender 1 cup chervil leaves and 1 cup water; pour the mixture into ice cube trays and freeze. When chervil is needed for cooking, just remove an ice cube and place in sauces or stews. Note: It should be added to the end of the required cooking time because it will become bitter if cooked in dishes too long.

Uses: Culinary herb (leaves, stems, and roots), can be used in stews, soups and sauces.

Apple mint; see *Mentha*

Armoracia rusticana (ar-mor-AY-see-a) **horseradish**, easy, perennial. ○ 🍴
Zones: 5 to 8
Height: 3 feet
Characteristics: Horseradish has wavy, coarse, large leaves 2 to 3 feet long. The flowers, which appear on 3-foot stalks in summer, are tiny and lightly scented. Once used as a medicinal herb

to treat stiffness, neuralgia and pain, today horseradish is cultivated for its root, used as a culinary condiment. The crushed root of horseradish has a sharp, mustardlike taste. Once horseradish is established, it is difficult to eradicate; if any of its thick, white taproot or numerous branching side roots is left in the soil, it can sprout into a new plant. It is best grown in tubs or with wire mesh as a barrier. Horseradish is native to eastern Europe and cultivated throughout North America.

Cultural Information: Horseradish prefers moist soil, containing a healthy amount of organic matter such as well-rotted manure or compost. Plant the root cuttings in the spring, spaced 10 to 15 inches apart with the thick ends up, 3 to 4 inches below ground level. It may be advisable to grow horseradish in tubs as it can be weedy.

Harvest: Dig the roots in late fall after a cold spell when they are tastiest and store in moist sand in a basement or cool spot. Roots will also keep in a refrigerator crisper for six weeks or longer.

Uses: Culinary herb, uncooked leaves can be used in salads; roots can be used to make condiments.

Artemisia (ar-tay-MIS-ee-a) **tarragon, wormwood, southernwood**, Native American, easy, perennial. ○ ◑ 💧 ☀ 🐛 🍴 🌱
Zones: Tarragon 5 to 10, wormwood 3 to 10, southernwood 4 to 8
Height: Tarragon 1½ to 2 feet, wormwood 2½ feet, southernwood 5 feet
Characteristics: There are three

popular herbs in the *Artemisia* family: tarragon, wormwood and southernwood. Tarragon is chiefly a culinary herb whereas wormwood and southernwood are grown for their attractive, aromatic foliage.

Tarragon (*A. Dracunculus*) is French tarragon, a shrubby plant with long narrow leaves, pointed at the tips and dark green in color, with tiny, round whitish green flowers. This is the tarragon used in cooking and shouldn't be confused with Russian tarragon, available often at nurseries but it has no flavor. Because the two tarragons are frequently confused, we recommend propagation by cuttings or root division to ensure getting the proper variety. Russian tarragon is native to Siberia and widely cultivated in Europe, Asia and the United States.

Wormwood (*A. Absinthium*) is the best-known *Artemisia*. It is a wonderful ornamental herb, with attractive gray-green foliage. Wormwood grows on stalks covered with fine, silky hairs. The leaves are round, 1½ to 4 inches long in fingerlike segments and have a distinctive, acid aroma. The flowers bloom in July and August: small round florets, greenish yellow in color. Wormwood is a very hardy plant that can withstand frost. It is native to Europe and naturalized in many parts of North America.

Southernwood (*A. Abrotanum*) has gray-green feathery foliage. It makes a handsome backdrop for the more colorful garden flowers. It has small flowers that bloom in August and is a heat-tolerant plant that easily withstands summer temperatures.

Cultural Information: Tarragon likes sandy, well-drained soil as it prefers dry conditions. Consequently, good drainage is a must. A yearly topdressing of compost in early spring will increase production. Propagate new plants by root division in early spring or rooted stem cuttings in the fall. Be careful of seeds sold commercially because these are usually Russian tarragon and not flavorful. Dig up and divide every three years to avoid overcrowded roots. Replant immediately at the same depth.

Wormwood prefers well-drained loam, but will grow well in any garden soil. Seeds are tiny but germinate easily and can be direct sown in fall or started in late winter in flats. Wormwood can also be propagated by cuttings in March or October.

Southernwood requires average, well-drained soil and full sun. Propagate by root division in spring or fall. Space the plants 2 feet apart. Prune in spring to keep shapely. Southernwood is native to southern Europe.

Harvest: Harvest fresh leaves any time. To dry for winter use, cut back the plant to 3 inches from the ground in the summer and again in early fall. Tie the stems into loose bunches and hang in the drying room. Store the dried leaves in airtight containers.

Uses: Tarragon: culinary herb, can be used in sauces, dressings and chicken and veal dishes and to flavor vinegar. Wormwood: aromatic herb, can be used as an effective insect repellent, add to sachets to repel moths; can be used as a companion plant to control black flea beetles and slugs. Southernwood: aromatic herb, the oil absinthol can be used as an insect repellent; crushed leaves can be used as a moth repellent; ornamental herb, can be used in a border.

Balm; see *Melissa*

Barbarea vulgaris (barbar-EE-a) **winter cress, upland cress,** easy, biennial. ○ 🍴 🫖

Zones: 3 to 7
Height: 5 to 8 inches
Characteristics: Winter cress is a member of the mustard family. During warm spells in winter months it achieves most of its growth. The branching leaves that stems produce are divided into five pairs of long lobes. These tasty leaves are a hot, spicy version of watercress. Winter cress flowers are bright yellow and bloom from March to May.

Cultural Information: Cress likes very fertile, moist soil. It is easy to grow from seed, which germinates in 4 to 10 days. Sow every two weeks to ensure a continuous fresh supply. Conserve moisture by frequent tillage, and water only when needed.

Harvest: Harvest while very young, using scissors to cut a fresh supply from top growth. Cress can be grown like leaf lettuce and is ready to pick in 50 days.

Uses: Culinary herb, can be used in salads, used as a garnish or cooked like spinach.

Basil; see *Ocimum*

Bay; see *Laurus*

Artemisia Dracunculus

Barbarea vulgaris

Bay, sweet; see *Laurus*

Bay leaf; see *Laurus*

Bee balm; see *Monarda*

Beefsteak plant; see *Perilla*

Bergamot; see *Monarda*

Bible leaf; see *Chrysanthemum Balsamita tanacetoides*

Borage; see *Borago*

Borago officinalis

Calendula officinalis *'Dwarf Gem Mixed'*

Borago officinalis (bo-RAY-go) **borage,** easy, annual. ○ ◑ ⫪ ⊕

Height: 1½ to 3 feet

Characteristics: Borage has a delightfully informal look and is at home in natural or meadow gardens. It has a hairy stem and attractive greenish gray leaves that are coarse, fuzzy and have the flavor of cucumber. The flowers, which bloom in midsummer, are star shaped in shades of palest pink to deep blue. It is a showy plant that can grow 3 feet in width and height. Borage is reputed to strengthen any neighboring plant, so interplant it in your vegetable, herb or natural meadow garden. Plant borage near strawberries where it will encourage their growth and hardiness. It also makes a great container plant to winter on a sunny windowsill. It has been called the "herb of gladness." Roman soldiers drank wine with borage flowers in it for courage.

Cultural Information: Borage will tolerate poor, dry soil, but grows best in compost-enriched soil with good drainage. Propagate by sowing seed in early spring. Germination takes 14 days at temperatures of 70°F. In early spring, sow the seeds directly in the garden. In the same season the plants will self-sow and new plants will appear in late summer. Self-sown plants seem even more brilliant. Thin plants to a distance of 2 feet. Use mulch to help retain moisture.

Harvest: Pick tender leaves before the plant blooms. Snip off carefully as in picking spinach. Harvest young flower tips as soon as the first blue petals appear. Borage doesn't dry or freeze well, so for long-term storage, preserve in vinegar.

Uses: Culinary herb, can be used in soups, in iced drinks or with vegetables or cooked like spinach; flowers can be crystallized. Aromatic herb, can be used in potpourri.

Burnet; see *Poterium*

Burnet, salad; see *Poterium*

Calendula officinalis (kal-EN-dew-la) **pot marigold,** very easy, annual. ○ ◑ ☀ ☣ ⫪ ⚘

Height: 12 to 18 inches

Characteristics: Calendula is an ornamental herb. It has vibrant, yellow to orange, marigoldlike flowers, hence the common name of pot marigold. The flowers measure 2 to 4 inches across and bloom continuously throughout the growing season. It has attractive, finely cut leaves of soft green that emit a distinctive odor when bruised. Both the flowers and petals of *Calendula* are edible. It prefers cooler weather and will often reappear in autumn and bloom right up until frost. Try planting near the brilliant blue of borage for an outstanding combination of colors. Romans believed *Calendula* to be the "herb of the sun;" they said it turned toward the sun and rotated throughout the day. *Calendula* has always been loved more for its beauty and brilliant color than for its medicinal powers. 'Pacific Beauty', deep orange, apricot or yellow, reaches 18 inches and is good for planting in the middle of a border and for cutting. 'Dwarf Gem' is a compact plant that works well as edging and in containers, with a lovely range of shades from lemon yellow, gold and apricot to orange.

Cultural Information: Calendula prefers full sun and light, sandy, moderately rich soil. This reliable annual is easy to grow from seed, but prefers cool weather to germinate, so plant seeds in April. They don't like to be transplanted so plant where they are to grow. Keep weed-free and thin to 9 inches apart. For continuous flowering, pinch off flower heads.

Harvest: Pinch flower heads off stems. Remove petals and dry on paper in well-ventilated, shady spot. Store in moisture-proof container. The flowers of *Calendula* dry nicely for arrangements.

Uses: Culinary herb, petals can be used in butter, puddings, soups and stews. Ornamental herb, flowers (dried or fresh) can be used in arrangements.

Caraway; see *Carum*

Carthamus tinctorius

(KAR-tham-us) **safflower, false saffron**, easy, annual. ○ ◗ ✸
❡ ⤳

Height: 2 to 3 feet

Characteristics: Safflower is a colorful herb that resembles thistles, with brilliant yellow florets that darken to orange in late summer. The warm yellow colors of safflower make it a welcome addition to any garden. The seedpods dry beautifully, holding their orange color. The native origin is unknown but this herb has long been known in Europe, Asia and, possibly, Egypt. Today it is grown commercially in Europe and California.

Cultural Information: Safflower likes a dry climate. Avoid excessive moisture, especially on leaves, as it may cause disease. Sow seeds in spring ¼ inch deep where they are to grow. Thin seedlings to 4 to 6 inches apart.

Harvest: Cut and dry the safflower heads in late summer and store the dried petals in an airtight container.

Uses: Culinary herb, can be used as a saffron substitute and to color foods; oil is used distinctively throughout India in cooking. Ornamental herb, dried flowers can be used in arrangements. Also used as a clothing dye.

Carum Carvi (KAY-rum)

caraway, easy, biennial. ○ ◗ ◖
❡

Zones: 3 to 10

Height: 2 feet

Characteristics: Caraway's carrot-like leaves are similar to those of fennel and coriander. Caraway is usually grown for its licorice-flavored seeds, used in cooking. The creamy white or yellowish flowers are minute and umbrella shaped. They bloom in June or July. All parts of the caraway plant are edible. Native to Europe, Turkey, Asia and India, but also naturalized in North America. Ancient Egyptians thought caraway had power to keep lovers together.

Cultural Information: Caraway prefers dry, light, well-drained soil. It is easily propagated from seed and often self-sows. Plant seed where it is to grow. It has a long tap root and doesn't transplant well. Keep the soil evenly

Carthamus tinctorius

Carum Carvi

moist but not soggy. Protect the plants during the winter with a mulch. Because caraway is a biennial, plant a new crop using fresh seed each year for a steady supply.

Harvest: Fresh leaves can be picked as soon as the plant is well established. Cut the fruiting seedpods from the plant before they scatter. Dry them on a white cloth placed on a tray or screen in sun or shade and bring them in at night to protect them from dew. To separate the seed from the stems, take the thoroughly dry stems and rub them between the palms of your hands. Store the seed in an airtight opaque container.

Uses: Culinary herb, seeds can be used in cheese, sausage, vegetables, meats, cakes and breads; young leaves can be used in soups, in salads or as a garnish. Ornamental herb, dried flowers can be used in arrangements.

Castor bean; see *Ricinus*

Catmint; see *Nepeta*

Catnip; see *Nepeta*

Chamomile, German; see *Matricaria*

Chamomile, Roman; see *Anthemis*

Chervil; see *Anthriscus*

Chinese parsley; see *Coriandrum*

Chive; see *Allium Schoenoprasum*

Chrysanthemum Balsamita tanacetoides

Chrysanthemum Balsamita tanacetoides

(kris-ANTH-em-um) **costmary, Bible leaf,** easy, perennial. ○ ◑ 🐞 ¶

Zones: 4 to 9

Height: 3 to 4 feet

Characteristics: Costmary is a sprawling herb that lends itself nicely to herb, flower, or natural gardens. The green-gray foliage has an aromatic, balsamlike fragrance with a mintlike flavor. The flowers of costmary are small, yellow clusters of tansy-like flowers that bloom from August to October. Planted at the back of a border it will serve as an interesting backdrop for lower-growing plants. Costmary was once called the Bible leaf because it was used to mark the pages of the Bible and its fragrance was called on to revive the tired churchgoer. Costmary is a native of Asia Minor and Iran and has naturalized in some parts of North America.

Cultural Information: Costmary produces little or no seed but spreads rapidly by underground roots. It is best propagated by division of its roots in early spring. It requires well-drained soil, but is tolerant of most soils from sand to clay. Place the plants 2 to 3 feet apart as they sprawl, quickly spreading to cover the ground between them. It will thrive in full sun to partial shade, but will bloom only in full sun. Enrich the soil by top-dressing it with compost in early spring.

Harvest: For best flavor collect the leaves before they start to yellow. The dried leaves of costmary will store well for long periods of time.

Uses: Culinary herb, leaves can be used in teas, iced soups and fruit salads. Aromatic herb, leaves can be used in potpourri (they also serve as a fixative to preserve the other scents); flowers can be used in arrangements and nosegays.

Chrysanthemum Parthenium

(kris-ANTH-em-um) **feverfew,** easy, perennial. ○ ◑ 🐞

Zones: 5 to 7

Height: 2 to 3 feet

Characteristics: Feverfew is a member of the daisy family. It has clusters of small, white, daisylike flowers with brilliant yellow centers, often confused with those of chamomile. The aromatic foliage of feverfew is yellow-green, like that of the fall-blooming mum. Common feverfew reaches 2 to 3 feet in height. A low-growing variety is available for annual borders, tubs and window boxes. Feverfew, as its name implies, was once thought to control fevers. It is native to central and southern Europe and naturalized in many parts of North America.

Cultural Information: Feverfew is a hardy plant requiring little attention. It grows in ordinary, well-drained soil and full sun. Sow the seeds indoors in flats in February or March at temperatures of 65°F. In June transplant the seedlings to the garden. Thin to 9 to 12 inches apart. In mild climates, direct sow after all danger of frost is past or in late summer. You can also propagate feverfew by root division in early spring or by cuttings made any time from October through May.

Uses: Medicinal herb, believed to help relieve migraine headaches (laboratory tests have in fact proven its effectiveness). Ornamental herb, can be used in a border.

Cicely, sweet; see *Myrrhis*

Cilantro; see *Coriandrum*

Comfrey; see *Symphytum*

Coneflower, purple; see *Echinacea*

Coriander; see *Coriandrum*

Coriandrum sativum (kor-ri-AND-rum) **cilantro, coriander, Chinese parsley,** easy, annual. ○ ◑ ✸ ⑂
Height: 12 to 36 inches
Characteristics: Coriander has slender, erect stems and tiny, pale pink or pink-white flower clusters that bloom from June to August. The top leaves are lacy and fernlike, but the lower leaves are broad and deeply lobed. The leaves of coriander have the unpleasant smell of bed bugs when crushed, but when the seed matures this odor disappears. Use coriander to attract beneficial insects like bees into the garden. Plant coriander near anise to enhance its growth. Once used primarily as a medicinal herb, today coriander is grown mostly for culinary purposes.
Cultural Information: Coriander thrives in poor to medium-rich, well-drained soil. Sow the seed directly in the garden in early spring. In mild climates seeds may be sown in autumn. Put seeds ½ inch deep and thin the seedlings to at least 4 inches between plants. Germination takes about 14 days, in soil temperatures of 65°F. Thin the

seedlings 8 to 10 inches apart. It is important to keep the area weed-free until the plants are well established. Allow the soil to dry out slightly between thorough waterings. Native to southern Europe, coriander is now found naturalized in Asia, India and parts of North America. It is believed that coriander has been cultivated for more than 3,000 years. The seeds of coriander have been found in the ancient Egyptian tombs.
Harvest: Seeds need to be harvested as soon as possible after they ripen to prevent scattering. When dry, they will fall out and can be easily separated from dried leaves. Harvest seed about 11 weeks after sowing. Harvest young, fresh leaves only for the best flavor. Dried leaves do not store well and quickly lose their flavor. Seeds should be well dried before they are stored in containers.
Uses: Culinary herb, sugar-coated whole seeds can be used as a confection; crushed, powdered and ground seeds can be used in liqueurs, gin and vermouth; dried seeds can be used in curry powder and to preserve meat; leaves (dried or fresh) can be used in Oriental, Spanish, Indian and Mexican dishes.

Corsican mint; see *Mentha*

Costmary; see *Chrysanthemum Balsamita tanacetoides*

Cress, upland; see *Barbarea*

Cress, winter; see *Barbarea*

Chrysanthemum Parthenium

Coriandrum sativum

Crocus, fall; see *Crocus*

Crocus, saffron; see *Crocus*

Crocus sativus (KRO-kus) **saffron crocus, fall crocus,** easy, bulb. ○ ◑ ⑂
Zones: 5 to 10
Height: 3 to 6 inches
Characteristics: The fall crocus is both an ornamental and culinary herb. It has 18-inch, grasslike foliage and a single star-shaped flower. Crocus foliage stays evergreen throughout winter, dying down in the spring. The saffron crocus has

Crocus sativus

been praised throughout history for its fragrance, taste and useful dye. The flower's stigma, the female part, is dried to produce saffron. It takes approximately 8,000 flowers to produce 3½ ounces of dried saffron, which makes it very expensive. For this reason saffron has always been considered a luxury spice; it was used by the Greeks to dye their clothing a lovely yellow color. It is native to Europe and Asia Minor.

Cultural Information: Saffron crocus grows from a bulbous corm, 1 inch in diameter. Plant the corms in fall or spring in rich, well-drained soil. It looks best when planted in groups of 8 to 10, 4 inches deep and spaced 2 inches apart. It will multiply or naturalize and increase in beauty from year to year. After a few years it is best to dig and divide the corms to avoid overcrowding. Division should be done in summer after the foliage has died back.

Uses: Culinary herb, the stigma (flowers' threads) can be used

Cuminum Cyminum

in rice, bouillabaisse, cakes, breads, cookies and Indian dishes.

Cumin; see *Cuminum*

Cuminum Cyminum
(KEW-min-um) **cumin**, difficult, annual. ○ ☀ ❖

Height: 4 to 6 inches

Characteristics: Cumin is a low-growing herb valued for its seeds. It has small, deep green leaves that are long and narrow. The flowers of cumin are small clusters of pink or white that bloom in July and August. These flowers will turn into the tiny pungent seeds, which are used as culinary flavoring. Cumin is native to the Mediterranean, Egypt, Arabia and Turkey where it is used as a popular spice and condiment for cooking.

Cultural Information: Prepare a bed of rich, loamy soil in full sun for cumin to thrive. Because it is native to warm climates it requires warm temperatures to germinate from seed. It can be cultivated directly in the garden, but it will take from three to four months to mature. It is best to start the seeds indoors in pots to be transplanted outdoors in spring.

Uses: Culinary herb, can be used in curry powder and Mediterranean and Mexican dishes.

Curled parsley; see *Petroselinum*

Dandelion; see *Taraxacum*

Digitalis purpurea (di-ji-TAH-lis) **foxglove**, easy, biennial/perennial. ◐ ○ ❖

Zones: 4 to 9

Height: 3 feet

Characteristics: Digitalis was once grown as a medicinal herb for heart ailments. It is still an ingredient in heart medicines but in today's gardens we enjoy this ornamental herb for its beauty. Foxglove makes a lovely addition at the rear of a border or on a woodland walk. It blooms on tall spikes with bell-shaped flowers in late spring and early summer. Most foxgloves are biennials that self-seed freely. *Digitalis* × *mertonensis* is a perennial form of foxglove, bearing spikes of bell-shaped pinkish flowers. *D. purpurea* 'Excelsior' is a biennial with large flowers borne horizontally all around the stem rather than the usual pendent blooms on three sides. 'Foxy' is the only foxglove that will bloom from seed the first year, approximately five months after sowing.

Cultural Information: Foxglove requires well-drained yet moisture-retentive soil, rich in leaf mold or other organic matter. Space 1 foot apart. Sow the seeds in late spring or early summer for flowers the following season. They can be started indoors at 70°F and will germinate in one to three weeks. Taller varieties will probably need staking. A second bloom in fall is possible if the stems are cut back before they are allowed to go to seed. The foliage of foxglove is poisonous if eaten.

Uses: Ornamental herb, can be used in early summer gardens and arrangements.

Dill; see *Anethum*

Echinacea purpurea (e-kee-NAH-see-a) **purple cone-flower**, Native American, easy, perennial. ○ ◐ ◖ ✹ ✿.
Zones: 3 to 9
Height: 2 to 5 feet
Characteristics: E. purpurea is an ornamental herb that resembles a pink or purple black-eyed Susan with its petals arched backward. It grows on sturdy stems with tiny, bristly hairs. It is a wonderful addition to any garden with its showy flower head 3 to 4 inches across. The lovely pink flowers bloom in mid- to late summer. The leaves are pale to dark green, coarsely toothed and 3 to 6 inches in length. The upper foliage of *Echinacea* is shorter and narrower. It was used by Native Americans to cure such ailments as rheumatism, bee sting and snakebite. *Echinacea* grows in open woodlands and prairies from Georgia to Louisiana, Iowa and Ohio.
Cultural Information: Echinacea is not fussy and will grow in any garden soil. To ensure fuller plants with more flowers, it is best to add some compost in early spring. This tolerant plant easily withstands hot weather and humidity. It is easy to propagate from seed. Divide every four to five years and enrich the soil before replanting.
Uses: Ornamental herb, can be used in flower gardens; flowers and dried seed heads can be used in arrangements.

Fall crocus; see *Crocus sativus*

False saffron; see *Cartha-mus*

Fennel; see *Foeniculum*

Feverfew; see *Chrysanthe-mum Parthenium*

Foeniculum vulgare (fee-NIK-yew-lum) **fennel**, moderate, tender perennial grown as annual. ○ ✹ ⑂
Height: 4 feet
Characteristics: Fennel, with its stunning clusters of yellow flowers and interesting filigreed leaves, makes an attractive border plant. It has celerylike, bright green stems and blooms from July through October. Use your fennel plant at the back of the flower, herb and vegetable garden. All parts of fennel are edible and have a licoricelike taste. There are two main forms of fennel: wild fennel (*F. vulgare*), which is a tender perennial grown as an annual, and sweet fennel (*F. vulgare dulce*), which is grown as an annual. Both plants have similar growth habits, but sweet fennel is more often used for culinary purposes. Plant fennel away from kohlrabi, caraway, tomato and bush

Digitalis

Echinacea purpurea

Foeniculum vulgare

bean, as it seems to inhibit their growth. Fennel is native to southern Europe.

Cultural Information: Sow fennel seeds in midsummer for harvest in autumn. Cover lightly with soil and keep moist for several weeks until germination. Thin to 1 foot apart. Because fennel can reach 4 feet in height it is best to place it toward the back of the garden or in front of a fence or wall to provide support if needed. Make successive plantings for a continuous supply. Fennel can also be sown in fall for early spring germination.

Harvest: Harvest fennel leaves any time after flower heads form, up until frost. Dry the leaves and store them in airtight containers. The seeds of fennel can be harvested when ripe in fall. Spread them on screens in a dark place to dry.

Uses: Culinary herb, can be used as a garnish and in salads; seeds (ground or whole) can be used in breads, cakes and cookies.

Galium odoratum

Foxglove; see ***Digitalis***

French parsley; see ***Anthriscus***

French sorrel; see ***Rumex***

French tarragon; see ***Artemisia***

Fringed lavender; see ***Lavandula***

Galium odoratum (GAY-lee-um) **sweet woodruff,** moderate, perennial. ● ⑾

Zones: 4 to 8

Height: 6 to 8 inches

Characteristics: Sweet woodruff, sometimes referred to as *Asperula odorata*, is an elegant, low-growing herb. When crushed the leaves smell like a combination of sweet hay and vanilla. In May a delicate spray of starry white flowers cover its impressive foliage. Plant it under a tree or in shady woodland areas where it will colonize and create a living carpet. This attractive groundcover has successive whorls of dark green leaves around its stems. As a low-growing, ornamental herb, sweet woodruff is a must for every shade garden. It is native to Europe and Asia. Sweet woodruff has become symbolic for humility because it grows shyly, close to the ground.

Cultural Information: Like most woodland plants sweet woodruff thrives in moist, well-drained soil. It requires a slightly acid soil, rich in leaf mold. No fertilizer is required when well-rotted leaf mold is worked into your garden soil before planting.

Harvest: Harvest the leaves and flowers any time during the

growing season. It differs from other herbs in that the fragrance develops only when the plant is dried. The green plant itself is almost odorless. Shoots are cut close to the ground in any quantity desired. Small harvested amounts should be chopped and dried immediately in a warm, dark place. Air dry only; an oven will dry it too quickly.

Uses: Culinary herb, flowers and leaves can be used for German May wine and in teas and punches. Aromatic herb, can be used in potpourri and sachets.

Garden sage; see ***Salvia***

Garlic; see ***Allium sativum***

Geranium, scented; see ***Pelargonium***

German chamomile; see ***Matricaria***

Germander; see ***Teucrium***

Ginger; see ***Zingiber***

Herb of grace; see ***Ruta***

Horehound; see ***Marrubium***

Horseradish; see ***Armoracia***

Hyssop; see ***Hyssopus***

Hyssopus officinalis (hiss-O-pus) **hyssop,** easy, perennial. ○ ◑ ⑾ ⚞ ❚

Zones: 4 to 7

Height: 3 feet

Characteristics: Hyssop is an ancient herb with a strong medicinal odor, and for this reason it has been thought of as a cleansing herb, used in sick rooms.

Hyssop is one of the oldest recorded herbs and is mentioned in the Bible. Today we grow hyssop as an ornamental garden plant useful for its beauty and durability. It is a scrubby perennial easy to grow. To create a full, lush plant, keep it clipped back to 6 inches, which will make it suitable for a knot garden border. It has woody stems and small pointed leaves that emit a pungent aroma when crushed. This camphorlike aroma repels bugs, and hyssop is rarely bothered by pests or disease. The flowers bloom in whorls of dense, ink blue spikes 2 to 3 feet tall in midsummer. Plant in front of yarrow for a striking color combination or near anise and dill for the wonderful contrast of foliage. It is not as invasive as other members of the mint family and works well interplanted in flower and vegetable borders. It is a beneficial plant, attracting butterflies, bees and hummingbirds to the garden. Native to Europe and Asia and naturalized throughout North America.

Cultural Information: Hyssop prefers light, well-drained soil. It is an extremely hardy plant and will thrive for years with little maintenance. Plants can be started by sowing seed in the spring. Thin seedlings to 1 foot apart. Take cuttings or divide in early spring or fall.

Harvest: Cut the stems and hang in bunches upside down in a drying room. Store the dried leaves, stems and flowers in airtight containers.

Uses: Culinary herb, dried leaves, stems and flowers can be used in teas. Aromatic herb, can be used in potpourri.

Hyssopus officinalis

Italian parsley; see *Petroselinum*

Johnny-jump-up; see *Viola*

Lady's-mantle; see *Alchemilla*

Lamb's ears; see *Stachys*

Laurel; see *Laurus*

Laurus nobilis (LAW-rus) **sweet bay, bay, bay leaf, laurel,** difficult, tender perennial. ○ ◐ ⅋
Zones: 8 to 10
Height: 10 feet (5 feet in containers)
Characteristics: Bay will not tolerate cold weather, but if you live in a warm climate like California or Florida you can grow it in your yard. This lovely tree will need winter protection in the North and can be grown in a container brought indoors for

Laurus nobilis

Lavandula *species*

Lavandula *species*

cold winter months. During warmer months it will make a lovely addition to a patio or terrace. Bay has handsome alternate, shiny, dark green, leathery leaves 1½ to 3 inches long with wavy edges. The flowers are inconspicuous, hidden in the leaf axis and greenish yellow in color. The fruits are dark purple or black berries about ½ inch in size. The Romans believed it to be a symbol of honor and victory. Heroes were adorned with crowns of bay leaves. Cultivated centuries ago by the Romans and Greeks, it is native to the Mediterranean.

Cultural Information: Bay is difficult to propagate from seed. The seeds need temperatures of 75°F to germinate and take four weeks to appear. One of the biggest problems in propagating seed is avoiding mold, so common to damp, warm soil.

Propagation with cuttings is usually more successful, but it often takes up to six months to develop roots. Bay grows best in moderately rich, well-drained soil.

Harvest: Pick the leaves and dry them any time throughout the year. Pick early in the day when the fragrant oils are strongest. Dry on a flat surface away from humidity. Place a weight, such as a cutting board, on the leaves to prevent curling. Drying takes about 15 days. Store dry leaves in airtight containers.

Uses: Culinary herb, can be used in bouquet garni, soups, stews and sauces. Caution: Remove leaves from food before serving because they remain hard and people have been known to choke on them.

Lavandula (lav-AN-dew-la) **lavender, fringed lavender**, moderately difficult, perennial.
○ ◐ ✿ ｜｜ ⚘

Zones: L. angustifolia 6 to 9 (provide protection in Zone 6), *L. dentata* 9 to 10, *L. officinalis* 5 to 10, *L. Stoechas* 8 to 10

Height: 1 to 3 feet; 12 to 18 inches for French; 12 to 36 inches for English

Characteristics: This shrubby herb has decorative silver-gray foliage and fragrant lavender flowers that bloom from July through August, making it a favorite in herb and perennial gardens. Lavender forms dwarf flowering hedges and is attractive lining a walk or edging a perennial garden. The fragrant flowers and foliage are the mainstay of sachets and potpourri. The flowers are equally at home in dried or fresh arrangements. Munstead dwarf (*L.* 'Munstead

Hidcote') grows to 18 inches tall and has silvery foliage and lavender flowers almost the whole summer. Lavender is native to the Mediterranean but has naturalized in the southern United States. There are some 28 different species of lavender. The most popular varieties are *L. angustifolia*, found in every old-fashioned herb garden with tiny clusters of blue to purple flowers; fringed lavender (*L. dentata*), with its green, fernlike foliage and blue flowers; English lavender (*L. officinalis*), with its blue-green, needlelike foliage and blue-green flowers and French or Spanish lavender (*L. Stoechas*), with needle-like, silvery-gray foliage and deep purple or white flowers.

Cultural Information: The plant prefers average, well-drained soil that is slightly alkaline. An infertile soil seems to improve the oil and thus the fragrance. To propagate, take cuttings in the summer in half-ripened shoots or sow seeds. Flowers in its second year if the plants are grown from seed, unless the seeds are sown early indoors, when there is a good chance for flowers the first season. The foliage stays all winter on the plant. In early spring cutting back the foliage to a few inches of the ground is an enjoyable task—you'll carry fragrance with you all day from having handled the foliage. Cut the dead branches back in the spring after the new growth begins. Spanish and fringed lavender can be grown indoors as potted plants in the winter and outdoors in the summer.

Harvest: Strip the flowers when they are in full bloom or as they open. Dry them in an airy, shaded place on trays or screens. *Uses:* Ornamental herb, can be used in a border, in fresh and dried arrangements and as edging. Culinary herb, flowers can be used in salads and other dishes. Aromatic herb, can be used in sachets to repel moths and in potpourri.

Lavender; see ***Lavandula***

Lavender cotton; see ***Santolina***

Lavender, fringed; see ***Lavandula***

Lemon balm; see ***Melissa***

Lemon verbena; see ***Aloysia***

Levisticum officinale

(lev-ISS-tik-um) **lovage**, easy, perennial. ○ ◑ ⑂

Zones: 3 to 9
Height: 4 to 7 feet
Characteristics: Lovage was once cultivated as a medicinal herb, but today it is grown for its culinary uses. It looks and tastes much like celery. It is a giant among herbs and can grow to 7 feet tall, providing a dramatic backdrop in the garden. The leaves are glossy and dark green,

Levisticum officinale

with a celerylike fragrance when brushed against. Lovage flowers are tiny, yellow compound umbels (clusters) that flower in June and July.

Cultural Information: Lovage needs a fertile, well-cultivated soil and lots of sun. Add compost or rotted manure in early spring. Lovage is easy to grow from seed or division. Sow seed in late summer or early fall; the seed must be fresh because it loses viability. Thin plants to 2 to 3 feet apart. For a bushy plant cut off flower heads as they appear. This will force the plant to grow wider instead of taller.

Uses: Culinary herbs, leaves, stems and seeds (fresh or dried) can be used in salads, soups, stews and sauces and as a celery

Marrubium vulgare

substitute; seeds can be used in pickling brines and salad dressings.

Lippacitriodora; see *Aloysia*

Lovage; see *Levisticum*

Marigold, pot; see *Calendula*

Marjoram, sweet; see *Origanum*

Marrubium vulgare (ma-ROO-bium) **horehound**, easy, perennial. ○ ◐ ✲

Zones: 3 to 9

Height: 2 to 3 feet

Characteristics: Horehound is the plant from which the famous horehound candies and syrup are made. It was once the only remedy for coughs. The horehound plant is bushy with wrinkled, oval, grayish green, velvety leaves 1 to 2 inches long. The flowers are whitish and tubular, growing in whorls above each pair of leaves at intervals up the stem. The leaves have a menthol flavor. The ingenius seeds have "hooks" that attach themselves to passing animals as they brush against the plant. This is the reason horehound is widespread, traveling to new spots where it acts like a weed.

Cultural Information: Horehound likes light, dry soils, but tolerates poor soils. It needs minimal water, so avoid planting where it is constantly moist. Horehound is easy to grow from seed but the seeds tend to germinate at different times—one may appear a week or two before the others. Cover the seeds with ½ inch of soil. When the seedlings are 6 inches tall, thin

to 8 to 10 inches apart. Once the seedlings are established, they will need little care. It will take two years to bloom.

Harvest: Cut small stems close to ground just before the plant flowers for the best flavor. If the plant is tall, take only the top tender parts. Two or more cuttings a year are possible in the northern states. To preserve, chop and dry the leaves immediately after picking, and store in a tightly covered jar.

Uses: Culinary herb, can be used for teas and candy. Medicinal herb, can be used as the base for throat lozenges.

Matricaria recutita (mat-ri-KAY-ria) **German chamomile**, easy, annual. ○ ✲

Height: 2 to 3 feet

Characteristics: German chamomile has an erect growth habit. It has the same daisylike flower as Roman chamomile, but with far less of an apple fragrance. Handsome feathery foliage with a downy covering makes it attractive in flower borders. German chamomile is frequently used to make tea, to relax and to bring on sleep. Because of its distinct aroma it was often used as a stewing herb, to freshen damp, musty smells, in medieval England.

Cultural Information: Roman chamomile thrives in sandy well-drained soil in full sun. Sow the seed in either fall or spring. Once established it will readily reseed if the flower heads are allowed to remain on the plants. Keep the soil evenly moist to ensure good flower production.

Harvest: When in full bloom, flower heads should be gathered and spread thinly to dry quickly in a warm place. All leaves and stems should be removed, unless you are drying the flowers for a winter arrangement. When the flowers are completely dry put them in tightly covered containers. Store in a cool, dry place until you're ready to use.

Uses: Ornamental herb, flowers can be used in potpourri, in arrangements and in a border. Culinary herb, can be used in tea.

Melissa officinalis (mel-ISS-a) **balm, lemon balm, sweet balm**, easy, perenial. ○ ◑ ● 🐢 🍴 🜄

Zones: 4 to 10
Height: 2 feet
Characteristics: Lemon balm is a spreading plant with heart-shaped leaves that are yellowish green in color and have stiff hairs on the top surface. The leaves give off a lemony odor when bruised. Try planting lemon balm in flower borders. Spikes of small white, yellow or pinkish flowers bloom from June to October. Some other forms are variegated lemon balm, lemony in flavor, and golden lemon balm has showy golden leaves. The genetic name *Melissa* means "a honey bee" in Greek, appropriate because the flowers are very attractive to honey bees. Lemon balm is native to the Mediterranean and naturalized in North America.
Cultural Information: Lemon balm likes sandy, moist, well-drained soil. Enrich soil with bone meal around the roots. Apply a thin layer of compost in spring. It may require water during long dry spells. Pinch the tops back for a fuller plant and for continuous bloom during the growing season. It is slow to germinate from seed and easier to propagate by root cuttings in spring or fall.
Harvest: Harvest any time during the growing season. Cut the tops back several inches as soon as the flower buds appear; this will give maximum flavor to the leaves because the plant won't be depleting its energy making flowers and seed. Cuttings can be taken two to three times a season. Early mulching with hay will prevent leaves from becoming soiled by any spattering of mud. It is important to dry leaves quickly to avoid blackening.
Uses: Culinary herb, can be used in tea.

Matricaria recutita

Melissa officinalis

Mentha (MEN-tha) **mint**, easy, perennial. ○◐●☀️ 🍴 🪣

Zones: 3 to 10 (pennyroyal, 6 to 10)

Heights: peppermint, 1 to 2 feet; pennyroyal, 16 inches; apple mint, ½ to 3 feet; spearmint, 1 to 2 feet; corsican mint, 1 to 2 inches

Characteristics: There are many varieties of this hardy, popular, fragrant herb, all with the familiar square stems. Mint has been a popular medicinal and culinary herb for centuries. It can become a nuisance if not controlled in the garden. Most of the mints emit a lovely scent when brushed or picked. Plant near the edge of a path or walkway where their fragrance will be enjoyed. Mint is native to Europe and Asia and is naturalized throughout North America. Truly one of the most aromatic herbs, mint has been used to freshen kitchens and sick rooms, strewn about the floor. Mint helps repel cabbage moths when planted among tomatoes and cabbage and enhances the flavor of both vegetables.

Apple mint (*M. ×rotundifolia*) is a vigorous grower. It grows to 3 feet in height with a reddish, hairy stem. The flowers are tiny and pale lilac in color. It is a hardy plant with the pleasant flavor of ripe apples. Apple mint can be propagated by cuttings or rooting runners. Add leaves to fruits, fruit salads and freeze in ice cubes to float in cold summer drinks.

Corsican mint (*M. Requienii*) is a low-growing herb that makes a wonderful groundcover for shady spots. It has an attractive carpetlike habit that looks nice on paths and between stepping-stones. Coriscan mint has tiny leaves, minute purple flowers and a delightful peppermintlike fragrance.

Peppermint (*M. ×piperita*) is a spreading, bushy plant with small, highly fragrant leaves light green in color and oval. Its flowers are purple clusters on long spikes reaching 1 to 2 feet.

Pennyroyal (*M. Pulegium*) is a prostrate creeping mint. It makes an excellent groundcover and does nicely in such informal settings as rock gardens, in herb gardens and along the edges of raised beds. The flowering stems, 6 inches high, have clusters of mauve flowers. Propagate by seed, division or layering.

Spearmint (*M. spicata*), milder in flavor than peppermint, is a bushy, spreading plant that reaches 2 feet with flowers from white to deep purple clustered on each spike. Propagate by division.

Cultural Information: Mint likes fertile soil that is deeply prepared and rich in compost. Work in bone meal in spring. Keep the seed bed and established plants evenly moist. Confine the roots or grow away from other plants. Can also be grown in clay pots. You can crack the bottom of a pot out and sink it into the garden to control the mint planting.

Harvest: Young leaves and sprigs can be picked and used as desired. Cutting them at intervals helps the plant grow. When the leaves are to be dried, cut them before the plant goes to seed. Place the leaves on a tray or screen in a warm, dry, dark place. When they are thoroughly dry, strip the leaves from the stems and store in a tightly closed container.

Uses: Culinary herb, can be used in cold drinks (iced tea, mint juleps). Aromatic herb, can be used as an insect repellent.

Mint; see *Mentha*

Mint, apple; see *Mentha*

Mint, corsican; see *Mentha*

Monarda (mo-NAR-da) **bee balm, bergamot, Oswego tea,**

Mentha spicata

Mentha piperita officinalis

Native American, easy, perennial. ○ ◑ ✿ ⑂

Zones: 4 to 9

Height: 2 to 3 feet

Characteristics: Bee balm is a favorite of the hummingbirds with its brilliant red, ruffled flowers. The bushy clusters of erect stems are topped with fluffy, dense heads of small, tubular flowers that come in pink, white and red and are arranged in whorls. The leaves are lush and aromatic when crushed and remain attractive throughout the growing season. Bee balm spreads rapidly, blooming from late June to August. They are handsome members of the mint family and, when steeped in boiling water, their fragrant leaves produce a refreshing drink, hence the name Oswego tea. Bloom can be stretched to eight weeks or longer if the flowers are removed before they go to seed. It is one of the few Native American herbs.

Cultural Information: Bee balm prefers moist soil, rich in organic matter and of average fertility. Deprived of moisture, the plants are more susceptible to such diseases as powdery mildew. In shady areas and rich soil, they become vigorous and spread rampantly by means of underground stems. Careful placement is important to prevent crowding out other plants. As bee balm spreads, its stems become sparse, tall and lanky. The remedy is to divide every three years. This will also ensure maximum bloom. Dividing is best done in spring. Space the plants 12 to 15 inches apart. Bee balm can be propagated by seed sown outdoors in spring or fall for bloom the following

Monarda citriodora

season. Germination takes one to two weeks.

Harvest: Cut leaves for drying as the flowering starts, to ensure the best flavor.

Uses: Culinary herb, used in salads, wine and tea. Ornamental herb, used in garden and in flower arrangements.

Myrrhis odorata (MI-ris) **sweet cicely**, easy, perennial. ○ ▮ ⑂

Zones: 4 to 10

Height: 2 to 3 feet

Characteristics: Sweet cicely is a graceful plant with a lovely, sweet scent. The foliage is pale green and fernlike. All parts of

Myrrhis odorata

the plant are edible and have a distinct anise flavor. It is grown mostly for its handsome, lacy foliage, an attractive addition to any garden. The flower heads are flat clusters of small white blooms in summer. The flowers are followed by large, shiny, dark brown seeds ¾ inch in length. The flowers are very attractive to bees. Many years ago sweet cicely seeds were crushed and their brown oil used as furniture polish. Today we use sweet cicely as an ornamental and culinary herb. It grows well in pots and containers.

Cultural Information: Sweet cicely needs partial shade and a moist soil. Prepare the bed deeply to accommodate the deep roots. In late summer or early

Nepeta ×faassenii

fall, direct sow the seeds, covering them lightly with fine soil. The seeds germinate after a cooling period of several months. Thin the seedlings to 2 feet apart. Sweet cicely can also be propagated by taking root cuttings in summer. To ensure success be careful that each root section contains an eye.

Harvest: Leaves can be harvested any time during the growing season.

Uses: Culinary herb, used in soups, stews, salads and bouquets garnis.

Nasturtium; see ***Tropaeolum***

Nepeta (NE-pe-ta) **catnip, catmint,** easy, perennial. ○ ◐ 🐝 ▮ 🍀 🍴

Zones: 3 to 9

Height: 1½ to 2 feet

Characteristics: Nepeta is a sprawling plant with small, coarse, gray-green leaves and 5-inch spikes of lavender flowers that bloom in early summer and often into fall. Their stems are square, a sign of its mint family heritage. Both the stems and the heart-shaped leaves are covered with a soft white fuzz. Cats love the musky smell of the foliage of *N. cataria* and will often roll, play and sleep on it, but the plants are tough and, though they may become matted, recover easily. *N. ×faassenii* stands 18 inches. It is a tough plant that makes an attractive groundcover. Propagated by cuttings or division because it doesn't set seed. *N. mussini* is the mauve catmint with upright, lavender-blue spikes on sprawling plants that bloom from May to September. Remove dead

flowers to promote heavier blooming. Besides long bloom, *Nepeta* provides interesting foliage color in autumn. It is native to Europe and Asia and is often found naturalized in America.

Cultural Information: Nepeta is not fussy and will survive in most soils with good drainage. A sandy soil will produce more fragrant flowers, although it tolerates both drought and fairly moist soil. The seeds of catnip are tiny and difficult to propagate. It is best to propagate by taking root cuttings in spring. Shear back plant in spring to encourage reblooming. Shear again in fall to keep shapley.

Harvest: As soon as catmint is mature, but before leaves start turning yellow, leaves can be stripped from the entire plant, cut and dried. Place on shallow trays in a warm, shady spot. When dry, pack tightly in containers and store in a cool, dark place. Two to three days are required for drying.

Uses: Culinary herb, used in catnip and tea. Cats also love to roll in it.

Ocimum (o-SY-mum) **basil,** easy, annual. ○ ▮ 🍴

Height: 1 to 2 feet; 3 to 3½ feet for camphor basil

Characteristics: The French refer to basil as the *herbe royale.* Basil is one of the most useful and decorative herbs, and no one should have a garden without it. It is available in many different flavors of highly fragrant leaves. The leaves are varied in color from deep to light purple and light green. Leaf texture also varies from puckered to ruffled to smooth. Grow several types of basil together for a tapestry of color and texture. Basil makes a perfect potted plant, providing wonderful fragrance for use on terrace or patio. Plant basil in your flower border or add to a window box or planter. Basil will complement your flowers with its color, texture and aroma. Native to India and Southeast Asia, basil has been a popular herb since the days of ancient Greece, where it stood for hate and misfortune, but years later in Italy it was a sign of courtship. Some forms of basil that are both useful and highly attractive in the garden are:

Sweet basil (*Ocimum basilicum*) is the classic basil indispensable for tomato sauces and salads. It is bright green and grows to a height of 1 to 1½ feet tall. The flowers of sweet basil are small and creamy white, blooming from June to September.

'Purple Ruffles' basil (*O. basilicum*) is an All-American Winner with decorative, ruffled, fringed, deep purple leaves that are both fragrant and beautiful. It has pink flowers which are also attractive but should be removed if the plant is to continue growing all summer. This is an attractive foliage plant, growing 1½ to 2 feet high, for flower gardens. 'Purple Ruffles' basil gives its lovely purple color to vinegars.

Lemon basil (*O. basilicum citriodorum*) is an attractive, spreading plant with pale, silver-green leaves with a lemon scent and flavor. It is used in potpourris, herbal teas and cold drinks. It grows 1 to 1½ feet high.

Bush basil (*O. minimum*) is a dwarf basil good for growing in a pot. It has a low-growing, compact habit with smaller leaves.

Camphor basil (*O. kilimandscharicum*) leaves have a strong camphor odor, sometimes useful as an insect repellent. It grows 3 to 3½ feet tall and has an equal spread.

Cinnamon basil (*O. basilicum*) resembles sweet basil but has a cinnamon flavor and fragrance.

Green bouquet basil (*O. basilicum*) is an excellent, decorative edging plant with a dwarf, bushy shape and tiny flavorful leaves. It is also excellent for pots and window boxes.

'Green Ruffles' (*O. basilicum*) has serrated, savoyed and quilted leaves much larger than those of sweet basil. It is a very decorative plant, 2 feet tall, and could be planted in the middle of a flower border.

Licorice basil (*O. basilicum*) is 15 to 18 inches tall with leaves reminiscent of licorice.

Ocimum basilicum 'Green Ruffles' and 'Purple Ruffles'

Dwarf Ocimum

Anise Ocimum

Cultural Information: Basil needs rich, well-drained or aerated soil and full sun. Apply water-soluble fertilizer monthly. Use of a mulch helps to keep plant moist during long, hot spells. Let plants dry out slightly between thorough soakings. Keep plants weed-free. Basil can be propagated from seed. Sow seed outside in May when temperatures reach 70°F; germination takes about 3 weeks. Basil grows little during cool spells so it is best to give plants protective covering.

Harvest: Fresh basil leaves are the most tasty, but dried or frozen leaves will work well in cooking. Leaves are usually large enough to pick when the plant is in flower but they can be picked any time; don't ever pick all the leaves as that will impede growth. To assure a second crop, keep the plant pinched back. Pinching back also helps to keep the plant's shape low growing and bushy.

Uses: Culinary herb, used in vinegars, soups, stews, salads, sauces, butter sauce for fish and is the main ingredient in pesto. All parts of the plant are edible and the flowers can be used as garnish.

Oregano; see *Origanum*

Origanum (o-RIG-an-um) **oregano,** easy, tender, perennial. ○ 🍶 🍴

Zones: 5 to 10
Height: 1 to 2 feet
Characteristics: Oregano is a close relative of sweet marjoram, with a more pungent flavor. It has a shrublike growth habit with broad, dark green leaves. The pink flowers grow in clusters and appear in August and September.

Cultural Information: Grow oregano in rich, moist or average soil. It doesn't require slow-release fertilizer if compost is worked into the soil. Sow the seeds outdoors when day temperatures reach 70°F; don't cover the seeds as they need light to germinate. Water only during periods of drought or when new plants are becoming established. Propagate oregano by root division in spring or by cuttings in fall. Oregano makes a good groundcover for a bank and is a good companion plant to help enhance the growth of beans. It is native to the Mediterranean and has naturalized in some areas of the United States.

Harvest: Gather the leaves to dry before the plant comes into bloom. The first tender leaves can be removed when the plant is 4 to 5 inches tall. Later, when the plant is well established, cuttings can be taken when desired.

When plants start to bloom, cut them back a few inches (this will keep them from going to seed) and use the leaves as needed. The leaves and flowering tops must be dried as quickly as possible. When dry, strip off the stems. Sprigs can be tied in bunches and hung to dry; leaves may be removed individually and spread on a screen in a dark, dry, well-ventilated place. Clean, dry leaves are pulverized and stored in tightly covered containers.

Uses: Culinary herb, used in salads, dressings, lamb, soups and sausages.

Origanum *species*

Origanum majorana (o-RIG-an-um) **sweet marjoram,** easy, perennial. ○ 🍶 🍴

Zone: 3

Height: 1 to 2 feet

Characteristics: An erect plant with clusters of white to pale purplish pink flowers. The gray-green leaves are woolly, oval and about 1 inch in length. Sweet marjoram is native to North Africa and Southwest Asia but has naturalized in Mediterranean regions. The Greeks used wreaths and garlands of sweet marjoram in wedding and funeral services as it was associated with joy and love.

Cultural Information: Marjoram requires well-drained soil that is not too rich. Marjoram seeds are small and are best sown indoors where they will germinate in 10 days. Set the plants out in the garden after all danger of frost. Water them well to establish the newly set-out plants and also during any periods of hot, dry weather. Weeds are fierce competitors for the soil's nutrients. Keep the garden area weeded especially during the first few weeks when the herbs are developing.

Harvest: Gather the leaves to dry before the plant comes into bloom. These first, tender leaves can be removed when the plant is 4 to 5 inches tall. Sprigs can be tied in bunches and hung to dry, or leaves can be removed individually and spread out on a screen in a dark, dry, well-ventilated place. Clean, dried leaves are pulverized and stored in tightly covered containers.

Uses: Culinary herb, used in salads, dressings, lamb, soups and sausages, for a flavor like mild oregano. Ornamental herb, used in potted plant.

Oswego tea; see ***Monarda***

Parsley; see ***Petroselinum***

Parsely, Chinese; see ***Coriandrum***

Parsely, curled; see ***Petroselinum***

Parsely, French; see ***Anthriscus***

Parsely, Italian; see ***Petroselinum***

Pelargonium (pel-ar-GO-ni-um) **scented geranium,** tender, perennial. ○ ◐ 🦋 ❀ 🍴

Zones: 9 to 10; elsewhere grown as houseplants

Characteristics: Everyone is familiar with the full, round heads and the many colors of standard geraniums as well as the ivy geraniums that are a favorite for window boxes in Europe. But old-fashioned scented geraniums, sold as herbs, are not as well known, though they should be. Probably they lack popularity because they are not as profuse in their bloom, showing smaller, more delicate, open flowers. As fragrant-foliage plants they are unbeatable, available with many styles of leaves from crimped, ruffled or curled, to deeply cut, broad, velvety or rough. When the leaves are brushed against, the fragrance released runs from lemon, rose, apple, allspice, cinnamon and wintergreen to "light champagne." The white-edged leaves of 'Snowflake' are so attractive that it's worth growing for its foliage alone, but it brings with it a lemon-rose fragrance. If fragrance is important, grow scented geraniums.

Scented geraniums are tender

Origanum majorana

Pelargonium crispum *'Prince Rupert'*

Pelargonium odoratissimum

perennials native to South Africa. They make wonderful garden or houseplants, adding interest to any garden or patio. Mass them together in the garden for a tapestry foliage effect.

Cultural Information: Scented geraniums require protection from cold temperatures. Propagate by root cuttings in late summer (see pages 27–28). Scented geraniums can also be propagated by seed. Dried leaves are perfect for potpourri. Keeping your scented geraniums in pots year 'round is an attractive way to display them and lessens the shock of digging up each autumn and repotting. Remember, plants in pots need careful attention. Water often and use a weak solution of a liquid slow-release fertilizer monthly during the growing season. Be careful not to overfertilize or plants will lose their intense

fragrance. Check that the pot is the right size for the root system of your plant. If you see signs of crowding or roots escaping from the holes in the bottom of the pot, it's time to transplant.

Harvest: The leaves and petals may be picked at any time.

Uses: Culinary herb, used in tea and jelly, candied to decorate cakes and other pastries. Ornamental herb, used in potpourri and nosegays. To candy the flowers, brush them with lightly beaten egg whites and sprinkle with a coating of fine sugar. After they have dried they can be saved for many months if stored in an airtight jar away from humidity.

Pennyroyal; see *Mentha*

Peppermint; see *Mentha*

Perilla (pe-RIL-la) **beefsteak plant, perilla crispa,** easy, annual. ○ ◑ 🌡 ❀ 🍴
Height: 1½ feet
Characteristics: Perilla is a tall member of the basil family with dark, handsome foliage of a purple-red sheen. The stems are brilliant burgundy-red in color. The plant has a delightful, spicy aroma that is cinnamonlike, but the fragrance is released only when the leaves are brushed or bruised. The inconspicuous, pinkish green flowers appear late in summer. Pinch off flower heads to encourage new bushy growth. A tough, pest-free plant, *Perilla* makes an attractive addition to any border. *Perilla* reaches 1½ feet in height and should be planted from the middle to the back of the border. *Perilla* adds interest in fall months when its color darkens to an autumn reddish color. It is a prolific seeder and provides enough seed to attract hungry birds. *Perilla* is native to India where it is grown for its aromatic oils.

Cultural Information: Perilla is easily adaptable and will grow in any type of soil. It likes full sun, but will thrive in part shade. Seeds can be sown in late fall or early spring. It tends to self-sow profusely. Thin seedlings to 9 inches apart. Pinch back when it reaches about 6 inches in height to encourage a fuller shape.

Uses: Culinary herb, used in tempura; the seeds are salted in Japan and served over sweets. Ornamental herb, used in gardens and flower arrangements.

Petroselinum (pet-ro-sel-LY-num) **parsley, curled parsley,**

French parsley, Italian parsley, easy, biennial. ○ ◑ ● 🥄 🍴
Zones: 3 to 10
Height: 10 inches to 2 feet
Characteristics: Parsley is a compact, bright green culinary herb with either curly or flat leaves. Italian parsley or *P. neapolitanum* has a strong flavor and a broad leaf. It is a better choice for drying. Curled parsley, *P. crispum*, is frilly and makes a wonderful border plant for edging. Parsley is a hardy addition to your garden and keeps its brilliant color and vigor even after frost in late fall and early winter. Try planting it near lamb's ear (*Stachys*) or sage (*Salvia officinalis*) as they also hold their foliage and color long into winter. The ancient Romans and Greeks wore garlands of parsley at banquets, believing it could help prevent inebriation. Parsley is native to Mediterranean areas.
Cultural Information: Parsley should be treated as an annual, sown each spring because the leaves become leathery in their second spring and the plants die off midsummer of their second year. Spring germination is very slow, often taking 6 weeks. To help speed germination, pour boiling water over newly planted seeds, or soak the seeds in warm water 24 hours before planting. Parsley likes fairly good soil enriched with leaf mold and organic matter. It tolerates cool soil. Water established plants well and keep them moist, but not soggy. Weed control is important especially while the seeds are germinating because plant develops so slowly. Parsley is a good companion plant for asparagus because it repels the asparagus beetle.

Harvest: Harvest mature parsley leaves as needed. Parsley freezes well and retains its flavor. Try freezing small amounts of clean parsley in plastic bags or drying and storing in airtight containers for use throughout the winter months.
Uses: Culinary herb, used in stews and soups and as a garnish and breath sweetener.

Perilla *species*

Petroselinum '*Extra Curly Dwarf*'

Pimpinella anisum (pim-pin-ELL-a) **anise**, fairly easy, annual. ○ 🌡 ⑪

Height: 1½ to 2 feet

Characteristics: Anise is an attractive, easy-care annual with creamy white flower clusters that resemble Queen Ann's lace. The flowers are sweetly fragrant and bloom in July and August. The leaves are light green, heart-shaped and coarsely toothed; as the plants mature, they develop a feathery appearance. Anise seeds have a sweet, spicy flavor and a strongly aromatic fragrance. Anise was once used to bait mousetraps—mice find the aroma of anise irresistible. Anise was highly valued by the Romans, who used it to aid in digestion and valued it so highly they would pay taxes with it. Native to the Middle East.

Cultural Information: Grow anise in poor, light, well-drained soil. It is best to propagate anise from seeds sown directly in the garden in late spring. The seeds need optimum temperatures of 70°F to germinate. Germination takes approximately 14 days. Thin seedlings to 1½ feet apart. Because of their spindly growth habit it is best to grow anise in a sheltered spot away from wind. A hill of soil can be built up around the plant as it grows to keep the plants upright. They need plenty of water during prolonged hot, dry days. Anise is a good companion plant for coriander, enhancing its flavor and growth.

Harvest: After the plant matures and blooms, the leaves can be gathered as needed throughout the season. Seeds harvested in the morning when dew is still on them will have the best flavor. Clip the clusters of seeds off the stem directly into a paper bag so they don't scatter on the ground.

Uses: Culinary herb, used in cakes, soups and stews. Anise is used to flavor anisette and many other popular liqueurs.

Pineapple sage; see ***Salvia***

Pot marigold; see ***Calendula***

Poterium sanguisorba (po-TEE-rium) **burnet, salad burnet**, easy, perennial. ○⑪

Zones: 3 to 10

Height: 1 to 2 feet

Characteristics: Salad burnet is a decorative, hardy herb. It grows in neat little clumps, lovely edgings for beds or borders. The foliage is sometimes hairy and has a distinctively cucumber flavor. This old-fashioned culinary herb is used in cold drinks and as a garnish. The rose and white flowers bloom in flat clusters on 2-foot stems. Salad burnet stays evergreen in all but the coldest zones. It is attractive throughout the winter months.

Cultural Information: Salad burnet prefers dry, poor, sandy soil and full sun. Relatively carefree, it requires no fertilizer or special care. To propagate, plant the seeds in spring or late fall. Thin the seedlings to 12 inches apart. To increase new leaf production, keep old foliage and flowers cut back. Salad burnet grows best in cooler weather.

Harvest: Harvest the leaves throughout the growing season. It is best to freeze clean, fresh leaves to retain their flavor. Divide the large plants in spring or fall. In northern areas it is best to provide a mulch to prevent root damage over hard winters. If salad burnet is allowed to go to seed it will self-sow. The plants are very resistant to disease.

Uses: Culinary herb, can be used as a garnish and in cold drinks and cocktails.

Purple basil; see ***Ocimum***

Purple coneflower; see ***Echinacea***

Ricinus communis (RISS-in-us) **castor bean**, easy, annual. ○ ◑

Height: 8 to 10 feet

Characteristics: Castor bean is a hardy, dramatic addition to your garden if placed at the back (so it doesn't shade lower-growing plants). It has large, coarse, gray-green or dark purplish red leaves. The flowers grow in

Pimpinella anisum

Poterium sanguisorba

tiers on terminal spikes and appear in midsummer. Believed to drive rabbits, mice and moles away from vegetable gardens, castor bean was often planted around the garden in the form of a living fence.

Cultural Information: Castor bean prefers a rich, well-drained soil. Plant seeds 1 inch deep after all danger of frost. If the growing season is short, start seeds indoors and transplant into the garden after all danger of frost. The seeds of castor bean are extremely poisonous.

Uses: Castor bean is used for its oils. The terrible-tasting, awful-smelling castor oil was once believed to cure childhood ailments. Today the plant is grown as an ornamental.

Roman chamomile; see *Anthemis*

Rosa (RO-sa) **rose**, moderate, perennial. ○ ♦ ❀ ✿ ❙
Zones: 4 to 10
Height: 2 to 5 feet
Characteristics: The Greeks called the rose the "queen of flowers" and indeed it is. The rose is the most popular flower grown around the world, a universal symbol of love and beauty. Some of the older varieties are grown not only for their beauty but for their medicinal and culinary benefits. The best roses for these purposes are *R. damascena* (damask rose) and *R. gallica* (French rose). They are both hardy shrub roses, highly fragrant and ancestors of our modern tea roses.

The French rose is 2 to 4 feet tall. It has bristly yet thornless stems. It produces large, fragrant flowers 3 inches wide in June and July. The flowers are a lovely crimson to pink, with brilliant yellow stamens. The damask rose often reaches 5 feet tall and has a climbing habit. It has lovely gray-green leaves and full red, pink or white flowers that bloom in early summer. The lovely petals of the damask rose seem to heighten in fragrance as they dry.

Some modern varieties of shrub roses are also very attractive and safe choices for the herb garden:

'Simplicity' is a hardy, disease resistant shrub rose that never needs spraying and for that reason an excellent choice among herbs and edibles.

'Bonica' is also disease resistant, with lovely pastel pink, double blooms all summer, followed by bright, orange-red fruit.

Cultural Information: Rose prefers full sun, good drainage and soil rich in organic matter. It also prefers good air circulation, as this helps prevent mildew and disease on the foliage. Rose needs large amounts of water, 3 inches weekly, but must have fast-draining soil. Feed in early spring and after the first flush of bloom with a slow-release fertilizer. A topdressing of well-rotted manure in late autumn will add nutrients to the soil. Old roses are very disease resistant and there is no need to spray the roses with chemicals. However, it is important to keep the garden clean and free of faded petals and fallen leaves. This garden litter is a tempting place for insects and pests to breed. If insects are a problem, try the natural defense of a sprinkling of onion water (cooled

Ricinus communis

Rosa *'Bonica'*

water in which onion has been boiled) or onion mulch (chopped onion green) around the base of the plants. Shrub roses need little other pruning and look best left to a more natural shape. Prune once a year in early spring or late winter before the buds appear. Simply cut out dead or old canes and cut existing stems back by one-third. Rose can be propagated from cuttings or buddings, but it is wiser to purchase your plants from catalogs and garden centers.

Harvest: Petals should be picked when dry in the early morning when the flowers are at their freshest.

Uses: Culinary herb, used in salads or candied for cakes and pastries. Rose sugar can be made by layering rose petals with sugar; let sit in a tightly closed jar for 24 hours or until the sugar has taken on the flavor of roses, then use the sugar to flavor cakes and custards. Rose water is made by simmering petals in water for five to ten minutes or until the water is flavored to the desired strength. Rose water is used to flavor deserts or as a toilet water or bath fragrance. Rose hips, the fruit of the rose formed in fall, are rich in vitamin C and are used in tarts, jellies, jams, teas, wines, breads and muffins.

Rose; see ***Rosa***

Rosemarinus officinalis
(rose-ma-RY-nus) **rosemary**, moderate, tender, perennial. ○ ◑ ▯ ※ ⌖

Zones: 8 to 10

Height: 2 to 3 feet (in Zones 9 and 10 it can reach 5 to 6 feet)

Characteristics: Rosemary is a showy and graceful plant. It has narrow, evergreen, green-gray leaves with a hairy texture. The stems are lighter green than the leaves and the tiny flowers bloom in various shades of white to deep blue. The variety *R. officinalis*

Rosemarinus *species*

Rumex scutatus

humilus has a low-growing, prostrate habit form. It blooms continuously throughout the growing season.

Cultural Information: Propagate rosemary by cuttings or layering. Germination is rather slow and risky from seed. Rosemary must have a sunny spot and well-drained soil containing lime. It will take poor soil but not rich, moist conditions. Rosemary is tolerant of drought and, once established, requires little watering. It needs heavy winter protection in northern areas, or it can be wintered-over indoors in pots. Because rosemary helps repel carrot fly, cabbage moth and bean beetle, it is a useful companion in the garden. Rosemary is native to the Mediterranean and northwestern Spain.

Harvest: The leaves are picked as the plant flowers. The plants may be cut or trimmed back two or three times during the season to collect leaves for drying. Dried leaves are crushed and stored in tightly covered containers.

Uses: Culinary herb, used in many dishes containing lamb. Ornamental herb, used in potpourri and sachets.

Rosemary; see *Rosemarinus*

Rue; see *Ruta*

Rumex scutatus (ROO-mex) **French sorrel**, easy, perennial. ○ ◑ ● ♨ ᛜ
Zones: 3 to 10
Height: 18 to 24 inches
Characteristics: French sorrel is

a hardy perennial with light green, spear-shaped leaves that have a tart lemon flavor. It features dense foliage and yellow-green flowers that bloom in early spring. Finches love the seeds.

Cultural Information: French sorrel likes a rich, moist soil. Sow the seeds outdoors in early spring and thin the plants 6 to 8 inches apart. Pinch off the flower heads to encourage leaf growth and to keep the plant from forming seed. It is quick to self-sow, and sometimes new seedlings appear the same summer they were self-sown. Clumps can be potted up in deep pots and grown indoors over the winter if placed to receive a minimum of 5 hours of light a day. Indoor plants will grow only 8 or 10 inches high, but that is enough for a fresh supply of leaves. The roots are deep and, once established, are difficult to eradicate. An organic mulch will help keep the roots cool in hot weather, and this keeps the leaves from turning bitter.

Harvest: Harvest the leaves as needed all season long. Sometimes the leaves become bitter in hot weather; the mild flavor will return when the weather cools. Use them fresh in cooking.

Uses: Culinary herb, used in many sauces, especially for fish and in soups.

Ruta graveolens (ROO-ta) **rue, herb of grace**, easy, perennial. ○ ✿
Zones: 4 to 9
Height: 3 feet
Characteristics: Rue is a handsome evergreen herb with metallic blue-green leaves, often covered with a white, flourlike

Ruta graveolens

substance. The lacy leaves of rue were grown centuries ago as a culinary herb, but many peole have a violent reaction when eating it, similar to poison ivy. It should not be eaten but rather enjoyed for its beautiful leaves and decorative flowers and seed pods. In most areas during winter months it will remain silvery; however, in very cold areas it will develop a brilliant bronzy color. The foliage can be clipped to provide a low hedge, but then it won't flower. The flowers are insignificant, small clusters of pale yellow-green, blooming from June until August. Plant rue in your borders, along paths and in rock gardens where it will delight you with its adaptability and foliage color. Try planting this silvery foliage herb next to white-flowering plants like foxglove, feverfew or garlic chive. Grow rue in your garden and you will soon see why it has been loved throughout history and often referred to as the "herb of grace."

Cultural Information: Rue actually thrives in poor, dry soil, but it needs good drainage. To grow from seed, start the seeds indoors in late winter and plant them outside in May. Propagate plants by cuttings during the summer. Rue does well as a container plant and can be kept on a sunny windowsill during winter months. Rue is native to southern Europe and northern Africa. Claims have

been made that it is a good companion plant to roses, but there is no concrete evidence of this.

Harvest: Harvest small leaves before flowers appear in the second or third season. Dry for winter use.

Uses: Ornamental herb, foliage can be used in arrangements.

Safflower; see *Carthamus*

Saffron, false; see *Carthamus*

Saffron crocus; see *Crocus*

Sage; see *Salvia*

Sage, garden; see *Salvia*

Sage, pineapple; see *Salvia*

Salad burnet; see *Poterium*

Salvia (SAL-vee-a) **sage, garden sage, pineapple sage**, easy, tender perennial. ○ ◑ ☀ ⑂

Zones: 4 to 8 feet
Height: 1 to 3 feet
Characteristics: Garden sage's (*S. officinalis*) attractive silver-green foliage is an essential ingredient in sausages and poultry stuffing, as well as for flavoring meats. It is a shrubby plant that grows to 2½ feet and has a sprawling habit. Flowers are purplish whorls at the upper end of the plant.

Pineapple sage (*S. rutilans*) can be grown as an annual or wintered over in a greenhouse. This sage is both fragrant and decorative. It reaches 3 feet in height, and has light green foliage that emits a wonderful pineapple fragrance when crushed. The brilliant, scarlet flowers are large and showy, blooming in autumn when most of the garden bloom is finished. Pineapple sage is not winter hardy, but it makes a wonderful potted plant. Dig up the plants in late summer and pot them for indoor enjoyment during the cold winter months. Tricolor sage, with its decorative leaves covered with splashes of silver, pink and green, is a plant I love to use; it provides interesting foliage colors and looks wonderful planted near silver- or green-leafed herbs.

Cultural Information: Sage prefers well-drained soil containing lime. It will tolerate dry, poor soil conditions, but not rich, moist conditions. Once established in the garden it

Salvia officinalis

is drought resistant and takes little water. In early spring cut away all the dead, woody twigs. Plants grown from seed take two years to mature. The plants are best grown from cuttings in early summer; you can also purchase plants. Set new plants 1 to 2 feet apart. Sage helps repel carrot fly and cabbage moth, and it is a good companion to both of the vegetables, but don't plant near cucumber as it will inhibit growth.

Harvest: The best quality leaves come from the tender young shoots (near the top of the plant) before it blossoms, but fresh leaves may be picked by hand all through the growing season. Sage leaves can be harvested in early spring and again in midsummer before the flowers appear. The leaves can be dried and stored in an airtight container for winter use.

Uses: Culinary herb, can be used in sausages and poultry and meat dishes.

Santolina Chamaecyparissus (san-to-LY-na) **lavender cotton**, easy, perennial. ○ 🐾 ☀

Zones: 6 to 8
Height: 1½ to 2 feet
Characteristics: Lavender cotton is a silver-gray, compact, evergreen herb with brilliant yellow flowers like tiny buttons that bloom from June to July. The plant has a musky aroma and is used in potpourri and sachets. Its low growth habit and dense, corallike foliage make it a perfect plant for low hedges or knot gardens. *Santolina* also comes in a rich green color (*S. virens*) and can be used in the same way as the silver-foliage variety. *Santolina* is native to the Mediterranean.

Cultural Information: Lavender cotton can be propagated by

Salvia rutilans

Salvia officinalis

Santolina Chamaecyparissus

seed, layering or cuttings. Sow in fall or early spring and thin to 12 inches apart. Or propagate by root cuttings or division in early spring. *Santolina* does best in poor, dry soil and a sunny location.

Harvest: Any time if grown for foliage. For dried flowers, cut at midday when their moisture content is at its lowest.

Uses: Ornamental herb, can be used in dried arrangements. Aromatic herb, in sachets to help repel insects.

Satureja (sat-yew-REE-ja), summer savory, annual, winter savory, perennial, easy. ○ 🐸 🍴

Zones: 5 to 10 (winter savory; summer savory is an annual)

Height: 6 to 18 inches

Characteristics: Both winter savory (*S. montana*) and summer savory (*S. hortensis*) are culinary herbs with a distinctly peppery taste. Winter savory is a delightfully tiny perennial herb growing 6 to 12 inches tall and about as wide. The tiny leaves form a dense mass and make it an excellent border or edging plant. It is the famed Bohnenkraut of German cooking, prized for flavoring beans, meatloaf and vegetable juices. The semievergreen plant has glossy dark leaves and a more pronounced aroma than the summer savory. Summer savory is a larger plant, 12 to 18 inches high, with narrow, lance-shaped leaves covered with soft, downy hairs. The foliage turns purplish red in autumn. Both forms of savory are dotted with tiny white, pink, or blue-lavender flowers from midsummer to fall.

Cultural Information: Both forms of savory have much the same requirements for growing. Plant in ordinary, well-drained soil. Summer savory, an annual, is best propagated by sowing seed in early spring. The seed will take 14 to 21 days to germinate; thin seedlings 4 to 6 inches

Satureja hortensis

Satureja montana

apart. Winter savory is slow to germinate from seed so it is best to propagate by root division or stem cuttings in spring. Space the plants 12 inches apart and pinch back the tops when the plant reaches 6 inches in height, to encourage a fuller plant. Divide winter savory every few years to encourage healthier, fuller plants. Once plants are established, keep them well watered during dry, hot periods. Mulch the plants after the ground freezes to prevent quick thawing and freezing, which creates root damage. Planted near beans, summer savory enhances growth and helps repel bean beetles.

Harvest: Savory leaves can be picked any time you need them. To encourage a full, heavy growth of new leaves, keep the plant fairly well clipped. In midsummer, cut summer savory at the soil line or pull up by the roots to harvest. To harvest winter savory, simply cut the tender tips during the growing season and, in autumn, clip down to 6 inches above the ground. Herbs are usually more flavorful before the flowers appear, so it is best to harvest for drying before the plants bloom. To dry, tie the stems in small bunches and hang them upside down or spread the leaves on screens in a dark, airy place. When thoroughly dry, the leaves are stripped and cleaned from stems and stored in clean, tightly sealed bottles.

Uses: Culinary herb (both species), can be used in gravies, stews and dressings.

Savory, summer; see *Satureja*

Savory, winter; see *Satureja*

Scented geranium; see *Pelargonium*

Sorrel, French; see *Rumex*

Southernwood; see *Artemisia*

Spearmint; see *Mentha*

Stachys (STA-kis o-fi-shi-NAH-lis) **lamb's ears, woundwort,** easy, perennial. ○ ◑☀✿🌱

Zones: 4 to 9

Height: 1 to 1½ feet

Characteristics: Lamb's ears is one of the finest of silver-leafed plants. It forms a dense mat of woolly leaves with a spread of 1 foot. Lamb's ears is named for its soft, downy leaves that resemble the shape and velvety texture of a baby lamb's ear. The tiny pink flowers appear in early summer. Once *Stachys* (or woundwort, as it was called) was used to bandage the wounds of soldiers. Today it is used as an ornamental plant for its interesting silvery foliage.

Cultural Information: Stachys likes full sun and a well-drained soil. It is best to propagate by root division in early spring or fall or to buy started plants. Seeds sown in spring take two years to develop into mature plants. Space 12 inches apart. This hardy herb will spread quickly, forming a tight, matlike groundcover, and will need to be divided every two to three years to prevent overcrowding.

Uses: Ornamental herb, can be used in a border.

Stachys lanata

Summer savory; see *Satureja*

Sweet balm; see *Melissa*

Sweet bay; see *Laurus*

Sweet cicely; see *Myrrhis*

Sweet marjoram; see *Origanum*

Sweet violet; see *Viola*

Sweet woodruff; see *Galium*

Symphytum officinale

Symphytum officinale

(SIM-fit-um or sim-FITE-um) **comfrey**, easy, perennial. ○ ◑🦶

Zones: 3 to 8

Height: 3 to 5 feet

Characteristics: Comfrey is a hardy, hairy-leafed herb. The leaves are lance shaped and often 20 inches in length. This impressive plant looks well at the back of a natural border. The showy, bell-shaped flowers hang in clusters of white, yellow, mauve or blue and bloom from May until October. Once considered the healer, comfrey (or "knit bone") was used to heal sprains and broken bones. Native to Europe, but it has naturalized in North America.

Cultural Information: Comfrey prefers fairly rich, moist soil. Propagate from root cuttings, division or direct-sown seed. Choose your site carefully because, once established, comfrey is difficult to move and even the smallest root left in the ground can grow. Comfrey leaves are helpful in the compost pile, where they will help speed up decomposition.

Harvest: Collect leaves in June or July to dry.

Uses: Was once used as a culinary herb for tea, leaves in salads. Recent research indicates the plant may be carcinogenic and it is not recommended for internal use. Grow as an ornamental.

Tanacetum (tan-ass-EE-tum)

tansy, easy, perennial. ○ ◑ 🐛 ✺ 🍃

Zones: 4 to 10

Height: 2 to 4 feet

Characteristics: Tansy is an attractive ornamental addition to your garden. The pungent, fernlike leaves were used as a stewing herb in the past but are now employed as insect repellent. This reliable plant is often seen growing along roadsides. It grows about 2 to 4 feet tall with an equal spread and should be planted at the back of the border and staked to prevent wind damage. The attractive blooms are clusters of buttonshaped, yellow flowers that bloom in mid- to late summer. Isolate tansy because its aggressive creeping roots can become invasive. Tansy is native to Europe and has naturalized in North America.

Cultural Information: Tansy will grow in any garden soil, but likes moist, loamy soil best. Sow seeds in early spring or late fall, or propagate new plants by root division in early spring. Space the plants 12 to 24 inches apart.

Uses: Ornamental herb, flowers can be used in arrangements.

Tansy; see *Tanacetum*

Taraxacum officinale

(ta-RAX-ak-um) **dandelion**, easy, perennial. ○🍴

Zones: 1 to 10

Height: 2 to 12 inches

Characteristics: It is difficult for most people to consider the dandelion anything more than a common garden pest, but once it was used as a source of nutrition and medicine, and European herbalists regarded it as a cure for anemia. This perennial plant with its dark green, jagged leaves seems to show up uninvited in lawns everywhere. The leaves are high in vitamins

and are an excellent source of nutrients. The dandelion flowers are daisylike, brilliant yellow and bloom in late spring.
Cultural Information: Dandelions thrive in deeply prepared, rich soil. They prefer cool weather, so direct-sow seed as soon as the soil can be worked. Apply a top-dressing of compost early in spring for a heavier crop. Segregate your dandelion crop in raised beds to control speading; dandelions are difficult to eradicate because of their deep tap root. Cut off flowers regularly to control spreading. Water well during hot, dry weather. The entire dandelion plant is edible and the leaves are very nutritious. Dandelion

is native to Europe and Asia.
Harvest: Use the leaves as soon as their size is satisfactory. Use a sharp knife to sever plants just below the crown.
Uses: Culinary herb, leaves can be cooked and young leaves can be used in salads; the hearts can be blanched and eaten; dried leaves can be used in tea; flower can be used in wine.

Tarragon; see *Artemisia*

Teucrium Chamaedrys

(TEW-krium) **germander**, easy, perennial. ○ ◑
Zones: 5 to 9
Height: 6 to 18 inches
Characteristics: Germander was once used as a medicinal herb

Tanacetum officinale

Taraxacum officinale

Teucrium Chamaedrys

for gout, fever, headaches and epilepsy; today it is used to decorate borders. Often called "poor man's box" because it was used in place of the more expensive boxwood hedges, germander makes a beautiful miniature hedge, edging or garden border. This hardy little herb also looks great tucked into stone walls or between paving stones. The glossy, dark green leaves are sweet smelling. The flowers are tiny pink blossoms that bloom in late summer. Shear the plant in early spring to encourage branching and to shape the plants when used as an edging. This evergreen plant spreads rapidly by means of creeping roots.

Cultural Information: Germander can be started from seed but it is slow to germinate, often taking 30 days. Try propagating by cuttings in early spring or by layering and root division in the fall. Germander prefers average, light, well-drained soil. Space 1 foot apart in slightly acid soil.

Uses: Ornamental herb, can be used as edging, a hedge, and in a border.

Thyme; see *Thymus*

Thymus (TI-mus) **thyme,** easy, perennial. ○ ◑ ◊ ☀ ¶
Zones: 5 to 9
Height: 3 to 12 inches
Characteristics: Lemon thyme (*Thymus* × *citriodorus*) is an ornamental herb. It has a trailing habit and only grows 6 inches tall, making a handsome groundcover. It has an intense lemony scent, emitted when the golden green foliage is bruised. Wild or creeping thyme (*T. Serpyllum*) is considered the first recorded thyme and for that reason is often called "mother of thyme." It is a very tough plant with a delicate, carpetlike appearance. It can tolerate drought and thrives in rock gardens, stone paths, and terraces. Wild thyme will grow to 3 inches in height, and its foliage is highly fragrant when bruised or trod upon. One unusual creeping thyme is woolly

thyme (*T. lanuginosus*), with grayish green, furry foliage (that looks as though it should be petted) and pale mauve flowers; it turns a burgundy color in the winter. Common or garden thyme (*T. vulgaris*) is the tallest of the thymes, reaching 12 inches. With pale mauve flowers that bloom from May to October, it is also the most fragrant and has the strongest flavor. Thyme is native to the warm Mediterranean countries.

Cultural Information: Thyme insists on well-drained, average to poor soil. Plants can be grown from seed outdoors in late spring. Thin to 12 inches apart. Germination is slow so it is best to propagate by root divisions made in spring. Propagation can also be done through stem cuttings taken any time. Highly fertile soil is not necessary, but a dose of dilute fish emulsion fertilizer in early summer will help the new plants. Trim back the plants in early spring to half the previous year's growth. Lemon and common thyme do well in pots

Thymus serpyllum lanuginosus

Thymus *weaves its way between stepping stones on a terrace.*

and hanging baskets. They require 5 hours of sunlight a day to thrive. Thyme doesn't like to be wet, so allow the plants to become dry between waterings.
Harvest: Pick the fresh leaves throughout the growing season. It is best to harvest just before the plant blooms or while it is in full bloom. To dry thyme, simply cut and tie the stems in loose bundles, and hang in a shady, airy place.
Uses: Culinary herb, can be used in chicken, meat, poultry and fish dishes and in soups. Bees are fond of thyme and they produce a particularly wonderful honey after feeding in it.

Tropaeolum majus (tro-PEE-o-lum) **nasturtium**, easy, annual. ○ ◑ ⑂

Height: 12 to 18 inches, climbing varieties to 6 feet
Characteristics: Nasturtium is a vigorous herb that comes in two forms: a low-growing, bushy form and a climbing variety. The nasturtium is a durable and colorful plant with edible leaves and flowers. Try planting some nasturtium with various scented geraniums for a handsome contrast of leaves. Its saucer-shaped leaves and helmet-shaped flowers are an attractive combination. The flowers bloom in a range of color from palest yellow to darkest burgundy red, throughout the summer until heavy frost. Nasturtiums look wonderful as a border for flower, vegetable and herb gardens, and make handsome container plants. Try planting some in tubs and tuck some into window boxes. Nasturtium is native to South America. Once the Romans believed that the nasturtium "sprang from the blood of a Trojan warrior," and the blossoms symbolized his golden helmet and the round leaf his shield.
Cultural Information: Nasturtium prefers average, well-drained soil. It is best not to enrich the soil too much, or the result will be lots of foliage and few flowers. Direct sow seed in early spring. Nasturtium is a good companion plant, helping to repel whiteflies and cabbage beetles. Planted around the base of fruit trees, it looks lovely and helps keep away harmful insects.
Uses: Culinary herb high in vitamin C, flowers and leaves can be used in salads; flowers can be used as a garnish. Nasturtium is a companion plant to help control certain insects.

Thymus *'Clear Gold'*

Tropaeolum *species*

Tropaeolum *species*

Viola cornuta
'Princess Blue'

Upland cress; see *Bar-barea*

Viola (VY-o-la) **sweet violet,** perennial **V. tricolor, Johnny-jump-up,** easy annual or short-lived perennial. ◑○❈🍴🐞
Zones: 6 to 8
Height: 6 to 8 inches
Characteristics: The violet family is a large genus that includes annual and perennial species. Sweet violet (*V. odorata*) is a most fragrant herb, used in perfumes and potpourri. This perennial has creeping roots. It reaches 6 to 8 inches in height and has heart-shaped leaves. Violets make an attractive ground-cover even after their flowers are gone; try them in woodland and informal gardens. The sweetly fragrant flowers are deep violet or white and bloom from March to May. Sweet violet is native to Europe and North Africa, and was more recently introduced to Asia and North America.

Johnny-jump-up is another *Viola* grown for ornamental purposes. It is one of the earliest violets to appear purple, yellow and white, and will often reseed and return year after year; it can reseed in the strangest of places, like driveways and paths. It has naturalized in some areas of United States. 'Princess Blue' is a lovely perennial *Viola*, a Burpee introduction that blooms from seed in 70 days. Slugs seem to like this, my favorite *Viola*. New additions include the Burpee 'Princess Cream' and 'Princess Purple'.
Cultural Information: Viola appreciates rich garden soil but will adapt nicely to any soil. Violets take two years to produce flowers, with the exception of 'Princess Blue', blooming in less than three months. In colder climates it is advisable to mulch violets. Propagate sweet violet by root division in late spring. The only thing that likes my violets more than me are the slugs; check Pests and Diseases for solutions to this problem (page 84).
Harvest: Pick the newly opened flowers of sweet violet for the strongest fragrance. Dry in a well-ventilated place and store in containers.
Uses: Aromatic herb; grown for its fragrant oils. Culinary herb, flowers can be candied and used as a garnish.

Violet, sweet; see *Viola*

Winter cress; see *Barbarea*

Winter savory; see *Satureja*

Woodruff, sweet; see *Galium*

Wormwood; see *Artemisia*

Woundwort; see *Stachys*

Yarrow; see *Achillea*

Zingiber officinale (ZIN-jib-er) **ginger,** tender perennial. ○🍴
Zone: 10
Height: 3 feet
Characteristics: Ginger is a herbaceous perennial grown for its aromatic rhizome, branched and knotty. The leaves of ginger are grasslike, 6 to 12 inches long and pointed. Ginger rarely flowers. It has an interesting flavor, a mix of spices and citrus. This

Viola tricolor

plant is not to be confused with wild ginger (*Asarum canadense*), an ornamental groundcover. It is thought to be native to India and southern China.

Cultural Information: Ginger is not hardy and should be grown as a potted plant in cooler areas. Plant the rhizome in a large pot filled with loam, sand and compost. Provide warm water and moisture.

Uses: Culinary herb, root can be used in sweet and savory dishes.

Zingiber *species*

USES FOR HERBS

CULINARY HERBS

Back in the 17th century they were referred to as the "sweet herbs," although I don't know how you could call dill, marjoram or chives sweet. Today they're referred to more accurately, though less simply, as culinary herbs. Each herb has a unique flavor and the ability to impart special flavor to food. Anise and fennel seeds taste much like licorice, but there are subtle differences. Caraway seeds also taste like licorice but are a bit stronger. Coriander seeds have a nutty flavor. Lemon balm, well named, tastes lemony and fresh. Basil can be substituted for pepper in tomato and cheese dishes. Burnet and borage remind one of cucumber, while lovage is like celery. Chive tastes like mild onion. Chervil is similar to parsley. Thyme is pungent, unique and rather indescribable; summer savory is similar in flavor, but milder. Sweet marjoram is a little bitter. Tarragon is sweet and not unlike anise. Rosemary is fresh and reminds one of pine.

Herb flavor is carried in essential oils that are transferred to the food. When you use them, remember the longer the herb is in the food, the more of its oil will be released, especially when heated. Getting the flavor "out" takes time, so don't add more herbs until you have allowed the first dose time to release its flavor. Too much of any herb is bitter. If you're cooking a soup or stew, add your herbs about 45 minutes before it's done. With cold food, herbs need to be added several hours ahead, even overnight. Savory seeds need to be crushed and soaked in the liquid called for in your recipe an hour before making up the recipe. Foliage herbs do not need to be soaked when the food is cooked a short time because the oils are readily released. They can be added directly to meat or stuffing or sprinkled over roasts. A word of caution: Herbs should help to bring out—not overpower—the flavor of the food. Until you are familiar with an herb, never use more than a pinch (less than ¼ teaspoon). The enhancement you're looking for is subtle.

Certain herbs enhance certain types of food. It's up to the chef to decide how much is just enough. Again, start with just a pinch and like any good chef, taste, taste and taste until you like what you've created. (It helps to keep notes too.)

Herbs, from top right: rosemary, marjoram, sage, tarragon and thyme.

There is great variety of foliage texture and color in the world of culinary herbs, from feathery to broad-leafed and from emerald green to elegant silver-gray.

HERBS FOR VEGETABLES

Beet: Tarragon, caraway, coriander, sweet marjoram

Cabbage: Caraway, fennel, thyme

Carrot: Parsley, tarragon, chive, rosemary

Onion: Basil, thyme, parsley, tarragon

Pea: Thyme, mint, basil, summer savory

Potato: Thyme, sweet marjoram, parsley, chive, mint, basil, garlic

String Beans: Rosemary, summer savory, sweet marjoram, sage, onion

Tomato: Basil, garlic, sweet marjoram

Chief Herbs Used in Cookery

Anise
Basil
Bay
Caraway
Chervil
Chive
Coriander
Cumin
Dill
Fennel
Garlic
Mint
Mustard
Oregano
Parsley
Rosemary
Sage
Summer savory
Sweet marjoram
Tarragon
Thyme

HERBS FOR MEAT

Beef: Summer savory, thyme, coriander, sweet marjoram, basil, garlic

Fish: Parsley and chive (garnish), fennel, chervil, basil, thyme, sweet marjoram, garlic, dill

Lamb: Garlic, rosemary, dill, mint, summer savory

Pork: Rosemary, anise, sage, chive, basil, sweet marjoram, garlic

Poultry: Sage, sweet marjoram, summer savory, thyme, tarragon

Veal: Sage, sweet marjoram, summer savory, thyme, tarragon, rosemary

HERBS FOR OTHER DISHES

Bread, Pastries, Cookies: Anise, caraway, fennel, coriander, mint

Cheese: Chive, caraway, sweet marjoram, anise, basil, thyme, mint, dill, sage

Dessert: Anise, sweet marjoram, mint

Egg: Basil, oregano, thyme, tarragon

Flavored Butter (or butter substitute): Anise, caraway, coriander seeds, chive, dill, garlic

One-Dish Meal: Sweet marjoram, thyme, coriander, caraway, garlic, rosemary

Rice: Parsley, sweet marjoram, chive, thyme, basil, rosemary

Spaghetti, Macaroni: Basil, chive, parsley, rosemary, sweet marjoram, garlic, oregano, bay leaves, thyme

HERBS FOR BEVERAGES

Cold Drinks (tea, lemonade, punch and cocktails): All mint (apple, peppermint, spearmint, lemon mint, to name a few), summer savory, pineapple sage, parsley, borage flowers, lemon balm

Hot Teas: Sweet marjoram, anise, lavender, mint, lemon balm, chamomile

Another traditional way to flavor stewed or simmered food is with a bouquet garni (herb bouquet). This is a small bunch of various cooking herbs tied together with cotton string, or placed in a cheesecloth bundle, suspended in pots of stew, soups and gravies for flavor. The herbs are removed before serving. Experiment with combinations for herb bouquets using thyme, savory, oregano, bay leaf, parsley and, perhaps, a clove of garlic. Get to know the most popular culinary herbs.

Herb Vinegars

Flavored vinegars give special zest to salads, sauces, marinades and grilled and sautéed dishes. Tarragon, burnet, borage (borage flowers will tint the vinegar pale blue), dill (add a whole dill head to the vinegar bottle), mint, lemon thyme and basil all make wonderful vinegars. 'Purple Ruffles' basil adds a strong purple color to vinegar and is delicious over fresh, ripe tomatoes. You can mix two or more herbs in one vinegar. For

Mint is generally quite invasive, so grow it in containers or use metal barriers to control its spreading.

a salad vinegar combine basil and borage or tarragon and chive.

Flavoring vinegar is simple. Take clean leaves, seeds and flower heads of fresh-picked herbs. Use about ½ cup herbs to a pint of distilled white vinegar, more for stronger flavor. Pour the vinegar over the herbs into a clean glass bottle or other translucent container, cover tightly and place in a sunny window or directly in your garden to steep for approximately two weeks. At the end of this steeping time you might choose to strain and rebottle the vinegar if you prefer it clear. This is also the time to taste and see if the flavor is strong enough. If not, add fresh sprigs of herbs to the bottle and let it steep a few more weeks.

Flavoring Foliage Plants

Angelica
Basil (Italian and sweet)
Bay (sweet)
Borage
Burnet
Chive
Lovage
Marjoram (sweet)
Mint (apple, golden, orange, peppermint, spearmint)
Parsley
Rosemary
Sage (garden and pineapple)
Savory (summer and winter)
Spearmint
Tarragon (French)
Thyme (all varieties)

Savory Seeds

Anise	*Cumin*	*Mustard (white)*
Caraway	*Dill*	*Nasturtium*
Coriander	*Fennel*	*Sesame*

Bottles of herb vinegar steep in the sun.

HERBS FOR VINEGAR, SALADS AND SALAD DRESSINGS

Anise leaves
Basil leaves
Borage leaves and flowers
Burnet leaves
Calendula flower petals
Caraway leaves
Chervil leaves
Chicory leaves
Chive leaves and flowers
Dill leaves and flowers
Fennel leaves, flowers and stalks
French tarragon leaves
Lemon balm leaves
Lovage leaves
Marjoram leaves
Nasturtium leaves and flowers
Sorrel leaves

Sweet violet flowers
Summer savory leaves
Thyme leaves

Freezing Herbs

Herbs most suitable for freezing are basil, burnet, chervil, chive, dill, fennel, parsley, sage, sweet marjoram and thyme. To quick-freeze, tie up small bunches of unwilted stems. Blanch the herbs in boiling water for one minute, then quickly plunge into ice water for two minutes. Untie the bunches, drain the excess water from the herbs, and pat them quite dry with paper towels. Seal them in small plastic freezer bags or cartons and freeze immediately. Chives and parsley may be chopped and put directly into freezer containers or plastic bags without blanching. It is important to label each freezer bag carefully because as the bags sit in the freezer, frost can obscure the contents from view. Freeze mint, lemon balm leaves and borage flowers in ice cubes for welcome additions to summer drinks.

Drying Herbs

The best time to harvest herbs for drying is midmorning, after the dew has dried, but before the heat of midday. Intense summer heat and summer sun rob herbs of their color and fragrant oils. Dry them away from the harsh sunlight, which bleaches their color, and avoid any place with high humidity, which causes mildew. Good air circulation is important. Remember, the quicker your herbs dry, the more color and fragrance they retain.

An attic, an unused closet or dry basement will make an ideal drying room. You can even spread herbs in a thin layer on cheesecloth or a windowscreen in a shady, dry spot. If drying outdoors, bring the herbs inside at night to protect them from dew.

Long-stemmed herbs like *Artemisia* and yarrow should be fastened together into small bunches with rubber bands. Hang the bunches upside down, leaving enough space between them for good air circulation. A simple drying rack can be made by screwing four heavy-duty hooks in the ceiling and suspending a piece of chicken wire from them. (The chicken wire can be cut into a square or rectangle to suit your particular spot.) Attach the bunches of herbs to the wire with large paper clips slipped through the rubber bands. You could also slip the herb bundles through the screen openings, flowerheads on top and stems suspended beneath. A clothes-drying rack or blanket stand could be used as a hanger for drying herbs.

For potpourri, tea or cooking, dry small leaves and petals. Place the leaves or petals on a fine-mesh screen. The requirements are good air circulation and a dry atmosphere. A simple drying screen can be made by stapling wire mesh over a frame (an old wooden milk carton, a used picture frame, a cardboard box, an old but clean window screen). Place the herbs in a warm, dark place. Drying takes approximately 10 days; if the room is humid, it could take longer, but fortunately a dehumidifier will speed up the drying process.

To dry herbs quickly, spread the leaves or petals on flat, dry baking sheets, set the oven at its lowest temperature, and leave the oven door open slightly. Bake for one to three hours, checking frequently. Your herbs are ready when they feel crisp and appear curled and free of moisture. Herbs may also be dried in an electric dehydrator, following the manufacturers' instructions.

Store thoroughly dry herbs in a tightly sealed glass jar in a dry, dark location like a cupboard. Direct light or dampness will cause herbs in storage to deteriorate. Crumble the leaves between fingers just before use, not before storage, to release fresh flavor when you want it.

POTPOURRI AND SACHETS

Once the air freshener of the ancient Greeks, potpourri was very much in demand. It was used to perfume a room, added to a mattress to help induce sleep, or was strewn about the floor to be walked over. Today we use potpourri to capture the fragrance of the garden, to bring it inside to add scent and charm to our homes. Potpourri enhances our lives with its delightful presence.

The main ingredients of most potpourri are lavender and rose petals, but other fragrant herbs, including catnip, costmary, lemon balm, sweet cicely and tansy are all good additions. combining different herbs distinctly changes the fragrance of your potpourri. A woodsy fragrance comes from adding pine needles, a citrus smell from lemon verbena. Display the potpourri in an attractive bowl or dish. Pretty bottles or jars can also be used; open the tops to enjoy the fragrance.

Sachets are another way to enjoy potpourri. They are little cotton or silk bags (silk's dense weave keeps herbs from leaking as they turn to powder) filled with dried potpourri, releasing their wonderful fragrance in closets or dresser drawers. In bygone days, people embroidered these little herbal pillows and sewed them into the lining of garments, upholstery and any other place they wanted scent. Some of the best herbs to use for sachets are rosemary, lemon balm, mint, summer savory, chamomile, thyme, lavender, marjoram, basil and the seeds of coriander, fennel and dill. Choose your favorite combination of these or add dried rose petals, rose leaves or cloves to selected herbs.

"Moist" potpourri involves mixing ingredients with concentrated herbal oils. Moist potpourri is made by placing thoroughly dried herbs into an airtight container, adding fragrant oils and fixatives and allowing it to sit for several weeks. The container should be shaken or stirred occasionally.

TO MAKE ROSE PETAL POTPOURRI

3 cups dried rose petals
2 cups dried lavender flowers
1 cup dried lemon verbena leaves
1 tablespoon powdered allspice
1 tablespoon ground cinnamon or cloves
¼ ounce essential oil of rose

Mix all ingredients together and store in an airtight jar for several weeks before using.

Rose petal potpourri

DRIED HERB WREATHS

Wreaths can adorn mantles, windows, doors and walls. Wreaths made with such culinary herbs as basil, rosemary and sage can be hung in the kitchen, the herbs clipped for use as needed. A simple kitchen wreath can be made entirely of bay leaves.

To make a wreath, use as your base a wire or Styrofoam frame, available at craft stores. Form the first layer of the wreath using fresh herbs that can be shaped easily to your frame. Larger-leafed herbs normally go on as the bottom layer with the smaller-leafed herbs on top. Lamb's ears and *Artemisia* are good for the base because they are fairly large and flexible, and their silver color is a good foil for the various shades of green herbs. Use florist's wire or clear fishing line to secure the stems to the wreath. Let the base dry in a cool, dark spot for several days to allow the herbs to shrink; this means you can fill in any gaps before the top layers are added. Next, wire small bunches of herbs around the frame to achieve the desired effect. The final step is to add groups of dried flowers or single dried flowers for color and a finished look; try yarrow or rose buds. Consider attaching groups of the tiny herb flowers: chive, sweet marjoram, mint and sage. For further interest, seedpods can be attached. If the wreath is for decoration and the herbs will not be used for cooking, a glue gun can be used to attach some of these smaller items. Your wreath can be as simple or as intricate as you choose.

An herb wreath made from sage, garlic chives, rosemary thyme, lavender, yarrow and rue.

HERBS AS INSECT REPELLENT

Certain herbs, tansy and lavender in particular, have the welcome natural quality of repelling insects. The pungent fragrance of tansy seems to repel fleas and bed bugs, and lavender reputedly repels moths. They retain this quality even after drying. Fresh herbs can be picked and tied in bunches to be hung around the house to keep insects away. They are useful, as well as attractive. Use the dried herbs of lavender, wormwood, southernwood or tansy in sachets to act as moth repellents in your closets, drawers and storage trunks.

Herbal Lore

Surrounded by mystery, herbs are among the oldest cultivated garden plants. Mysterious, sometimes magical, powers ascribed to herbs have fascinated humans for centuries. Just as we look into our medicine cabinets to alleviate various ailments, people years ago looked into their gardens for cures. Legend and tradition have long attributed many medical properties to herbs, some of which have been substantiated by modern science. The formulae for many of today's drugs were drawn from early herbal remedies. But herbs were also believed to have magical qualities, influence from the realm of the supernatural. Legendary claims include the following:

ANISE leaves applied externally remove freckles. Anise oil poisons pigeons, catches mice and combats insects.

BASIL keeps away witches. When dried and burned, it disinfects the air.

BORAGE fights fevers and acts as a stimulant, driving away melancholy.

BURNET heals wounds and infections, cures gout and rheumatism.

CARAWAY cures colic and gout, protects objects from theft.

CATNIP keeps away rats.

CHAMOMILE ends insomnia and calms nerves, repels biting insects. Compresses soaked in chamomile ease sore muscles. Rinsed through hair, it lightens the color.

DANDELION cures liver ailments and warts, relieves muscle cramps.

DILL stops hiccoughs and strengthens the brain.

FENNEL sharpens sight, wards off evil spirits and promotes longevity.

GARLIC treats asthma, hysteria, colds, scurvy and sun stroke. Crushed on the skin, it cures poison ivy and poison oak.

HOREHOUND eases sore throats and coughs, combats snake bites and poisoning.

LAVENDER added to bath water soothes nervousness, relieves rheumatism and gout, and cures head pains.

LEMON BALM braces the nerves, stops fainting spells and is good for headaches and colds. It renews youth, strengthens the brain and is used for surgical dressings.

MINT is good for stomach disorders. Rubbed on the table, it stimulates appetites. Mint cures mouth sores, whitens teeth, relieves chapped hands and repels mice.

PARSLEY is used as a diuretic, treats diabetes.

ROSEMARY is good for nervous headaches, trembling, dizziness and stomach disorders. It improves the memory, disinfects air and protects garments from moths. It is also a hair conditioner. A sprig under the pillow chases the evil eye.

SAGE remedies head colds and inflammation, and works as an astringent. It is used as a hair conditioner and darkens gray hair. Sage increases longevity, diminishes grief, stops trembling and cures snake bites.

SAVORY makes the old feel young again. It cures colic, clears eyesight, ends deafness, relieves toothaches and soothes wasp and bee stings.

SWEET MARJORAM is applied externally to heal sprains and bruises.

TARRAGON cures toothaches and the bites of mad dogs.

THYME eases muscle cramps, nervous disorders, headaches and giddiness. It is used as an antiseptic and fumigant, inspires courage, heals leprosy and cures whooping cough.

Note: Caution, Please—These are legendary beliefs among various peoples of the world. We do not recommend that herbs be used as substitutes for professional medical treatment, nor do we recommend use of any herb without expert medical advice. Some herbs, even in small amounts, may cause gastric disturbances or allergic reactions in susceptible people.

FRESH HERBS IN FLOWER ARRANGING

Herbs used in fresh flower arrangements provide not only the beauty of color and texture but fragrance too. Your arrangements may be tiny and simple, combining various foliage textures and scents. A small handful of scented herbs like mint, lemon sage and furry, scented geraniums creates a delightful bouquet. Or your arrangement may be as grand as an armful of taller herbs. The gutsy-scented *Calendula* and the sweet-smelling violet are pretty as they fill a room with fragrance. The pungent smell of lavender and the fresh, clean smell of mint add to the beauty of the bouquet.

Herbs, with their wide range of flower colors, make delightful additions to any arrangement. From the deepest red flower of pineapple sage to the brilliant crayon yellow of yarrow and the deep blues of borage, herbs come in a rainbow of choices. Explore the tubular flowers of foxglove with their interesting splotches of accent colors, bergamot with its strong red to palest pink flowers, the small, white, daisylike flowers of chamomile and the graceful sprays of catnip's tiny, mauve flowers.

Herbs offer more than brilliant colors and fragrance. They provide a variety of flower sizes and shapes, from the tiny, lacy clusters of dill, chervil and fennel flowers, to the pompom flower of chive and the flat-topped flower of yarrow. The textured leaves of velvety lamb's ears, the deeply divided foliage of lovage and the curly foliage of parsley add interest. For a lacy, airy look, add some *Artemisia* or the feathery foliage of fennel. Use some of the creeping thymes or whorls of sweet woodruff foliage to encircle your arrangement. For taller flowers try combining borage and dill, and surround them both with coral-shaped leaves and the yellow button flowers of *Santolina*.

During Elizabethan times, nosegays—tiny, fragrant flower bouquets—were carried in the hand, ready to disguise the dreadful smells of city streets. An herbal nosegay will provide both color and fragrance to your table. A nosegay at each place setting is a charming way to decorate your table (and your guests can take them home as party favors).

How to Make a Nosegay

Start with a center flower, possibly a rosebud. Surround it with alternating rings or bunches of fragrant herb foliage and flowers. Use lavender, thyme, mint, rosemary and southernwood. Colorful herbal foliage additions might be tricolor sage, fleecy lamb's ears, and the lacy foliage of *Artemisia*. The last row encircling your nosegay should consist of only one type of foliage, preferably one with interesting texture like lamb's ears or sage. This border will help to hold the nosegay snugly in place and provide a pleasing frame. The final step is to cut a hole in a paper doily, slip the nosegay in and tie it securely with pretty ribbons.

An assortment of herbs waiting to be prepared for drying.

Herb Teas

Many herbs may be brewed as teas, but the most commonly used are lemon balm, catnip, chamomile, dandelion, horehound, rosehip and mint. Aside from their light and refreshing flavor, herbal teas chilled or hot offer a soothing alternative for people who cannot tolerate the stimulants and acids found in coffee and ordinary teas.

Centuries ago, teas were the chief way in which herbs were consumed for their medicinal and legendary magical qualities; today we use herb teas as much for their pleasing flavor as for whatever healing properties they may be believed to possess. A tea of angelica was believed to relieve indigestion, and chamomile at bedtime brought relaxation and sleep. Many members of the mint family had various uses, from apple mint for a stimulant, to peppermint to relieve headache.

Tea may be made from fresh herbs, although it is more usual to use dried leaves, stems and sometimes even roots. Fill a tea strainer spoon or tea ball with dried herbs. Steep the herbs in freshly boiled water for 5 to 10 minutes, depending on the desired strength. Usually one teaspoon of dried herbs is used for each cup of tea. Some of the stronger-tasting herbs may be reused to brew a second pot, but most herbs are best discarded after a single use.

For added variety in your cup of tea, combine several herbs in mixtures, such as chamomile, mint and lemon balm, catnip and mint, chamomile and horehound, or dandelion and lemon balm. Dried rose hips, the fruit of the rose, are frequently added to tea mixtures.

For a unique taste treat, you may sweeten herbal tea with honey. A cinnamon stick used to stir the tea also adds distinctive flavor. Iced herbal tea with lemon and a few sprigs of mint makes a great summertime cooler.

HERBS GROWN FOR TEA

Angelica
Aniseed
Balm (lemon)
Bergamot
Catnip
Chamomile
Lovage
Mint (apple, peppermint, spearmint and others)
Sweet marjoram
Thyme (lemon)

Note: While some of these herbs are considered useful for medicinal purposes, most simply produce a delightful beverage.

The Language of Herbs

Many herbs are believed to control emotions and instill a person with certain positive traits such as bravery and wisdom. Some herbs (basil for example), have two powerful, yet opposite, meanings. Eventually herbs became symbols of these mysterious powers and were closely associated to their symbols. Gifts of certain herbs carry intended messages. Unspoken messages were given to the receiver by the gift of the appropriate herb.

Herbs	Symbols
Allium	The universe
Balm	Sympathy (lemon)
Basil	Love and hate
Borage	Courage
Burnet	A merry heart
Calendula	Grief
Chamomile	Patience in adversity
Costmary	Impatience

Herbs	Symbols
Dill	Lull to sleep
Horehound	Health
Mint	Wisdom
Rosemary	Remembrance
Sage	Immortality and domestic virtue
Sweet marjoram	Happiness
Tarragon	To share
Thyme	Bravery

PESTS AND DISEASES

Herbs are luckier than most other garden plants in that many of them have built-in protection against insects. Their fragrance, sometimes pungent, sometimes aromatic, the very fragrance that delights humans, seems to drive away many pesky garden insects. Many herbs help protect their immediate garden neighbors by this means. Tansy and feverfew have been used as insect repellents inside the home as well as in the garden. Some marigolds emit a strong aroma that repels and destroys soil-bound pests; for this reason they work well when interplanted with tomatoes and potatoes. Members of the onion family are pest repellents to various degrees. The clippings from onion tops or chive can be scattered around rose bushes as mulch to drive away insects and cut down on black spot. Thyme, savory, hyssop, sweet marjoram, sage and rosemary are all enjoyed by the bees and butterflies, and these insects in turn deter flies and beetles, creating a healthy atmosphere in the garden.

At Burpee we feel that the safest way to approach pest and disease control is through prevention. By taking simple garden housekeeping steps before troubles arise, you can prevent many problems. Here are some of the basic requirements of healthy, happy herbs.

First, provide your herbs with the healthy soil conditions they require. Healthy weed- and disease-free soil produces strong plants that can ward off insect and disease attacks. Keep the garden free of weeds and other garden litter. Litter is a favorite hiding place of garden pests. Finally, provide the proper drainage for your herbs. This will eliminate stagnant water, a prolific breeding place for insects.

The natural approach to pest and disease control is especially important in the herb garden. Remember that, like the vegetables you grow, many herbs are edible and should not be sprayed with dangerous chemicals. Such chemicals, with their initial advantages, are causing long-range ill effects to our planet. Chemicals seep into our water supply and affect our health. Chemicals have created an imbalance in nature. One harmful side effect of poisonous chemicals is the disappearance of beneficial insects, birds and other garden friends. Our goal at Burpee is to return the delicate balance of nature to normal. When balance is achieved, the garden will safely control most unwanted insects and pests by itself. Invite beneficial insects into your garden. These garden friends can be ordered from Burpee and other garden companies. Ladybugs, green lacewings and praying mantises are shipped to you ready to clean up the unwanted garden pests. These tiny garden soldiers can consume several times their weight in harmful insects every day and virtually eliminate the need for chemicals.

Another safe and easy way to combat some insect problems is to simply use a strong spray of water. This method will usually wash off an infestation of aphids. If something stronger is needed, try an environmentally sound product like Ringer's or Safer's insecticidal soap. Spray a solution of this concentrated soapy product on affected plants and repeat every three days until the insects are gone. Watch for up to three weeks, because eggs can continue to hatch until this point. It is important to follow directions carefully.

Detection: Check your plants for disease and insects regularly. Sometimes you will need to use some of the remedies mentioned above. Remember that you can't always solve the problem entirely. Sometimes it is best to dispose of a diseased plant; remember to place it in the trash can, not the mulch pile, where it could spread disease.

Quick treatment: Act quickly, at the first sign of disease or insects. The faster you act, the better your chance of solving the problem. Some common herb garden pests include:

APHIDS (APHIS): These pear-shaped insects are variously colored. Aphids have long, slender beaks that pierce the plant tissue so the insects can suck the sap. Aphids come about 10 to the inch. They multiply very quickly and can destroy a plant almost overnight. They also spread disease. However, they are fragile and suffer high mortality. You can help them to even higher mortality by spraying infected plants with a solution of Safer's Insecticidal Soap or soapy water (two tablespoons of liquid dishwashing detergent per gallon of water.) The higher the pressure of the spray, the more you can dilute the soapy solution and have it still be effective. In the case of a houseplant, you need only wipe the leaves with soapy solution. Wash the soap away completely after treatment to avoid damaging the leaves. If you spot ants around the plants, this is usually a sign that aphids are present. Ants feed on the honeydew that aphids secrete.

Prevention: Keep their natural enemies around: ladybugs, praying mantises, and green lacewings.

Aphids

SLUGS AND SNAILS: Easy to spot, snails grow to 1½ inches and slugs to 5 inches long. The difference is that snails are clothed with a shell and slugs are naked. They sport the same colors: black, brown, gray, tan or yellow. Both attack the foliage where they chew holes. They leave a telltale trail of slime as they move.

Prevention: Wood ashes, lime or diatomaceous soil (coarse earth made from silica-rich diatom shells) spread around the base of susceptible plants or the perimeter of the garden is often helpful. Slugs crawling over soil, very rough in texture, are torn open and die. Disgusting, but very effective. These products are safe but may need to be reapplied after every rain.

Ladybug

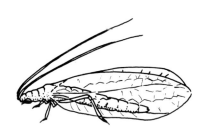

Green lacewing

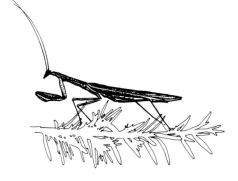

Praying mantis

Leaves damaged by the following pests, from left: beetles, flea beetles, caterpillars, aphids and leafhoppers.

Beer traps are an effective treatment. They, too, lose their effectiveness after rain and need to be replaced often. To make a beer trap, simply sink a shallow dish or pan into the garden with its rim at soil level and fill with beer. The slugs are drawn by the yeast smell, and will crawl into the beer and drown. If you don't want to waste money on beer for slugs, you can make your own liquid bait.

LIQUID SLUG BAIT

1 cup water
1 teaspoon sugar
¼ teaspoon yeast

Mix until well combined.

WHITEFLY: Whiteflies grow to ¹⁄₁₆ inch and have very large white wings for their size. They suck plant leaves, which turn yellow and eventually drop off, weakening the plant. They also carry diseases.

Prevention: Yellow pest strips coated with oil are available. The whiteflies are attracted to the yellow color and stick to the strips. This is a fairly effective and pleasant way to control numbers of whiteflies, if you can manage to hang the strips discretely out of sight. Good spacing as specified for the plant variety should be provided when planting, so that air can circulate freely. More space between plants means less room for insects to hide and breed.

Slug

Snail

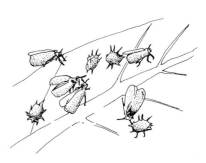

Whiteflies

PROBLEMS INDOORS

Red spider mite

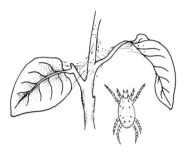

Spider mite

The close and dry conditions of many homes can bring such problems as spider mites, whiteflies and aphids on succulent plants, and scale on woody plants. Use a soap spray to control the spider mites, whiteflies and aphids. You can use commercial products like Safer's, or dissolve one to two tablespoons of a flaked, mild soap like Ivory in a gallon of warm (not hot) water. Spray every three days until the plants are brought under control. Continue to check plants for insects as eggs can hatch up to three weeks. Don't neglect the underside of the leaves. That's where the insects like to do their damage. Be sure to wash off the soapy residue before you add the leaves to your food.

Scale can be controlled by scraping off the insects or by daubing them weekly with alcohol-dipped cotton swabs. Always isolate any infested plants. I put mine in my plant hospital in a corner of the garage. If you are unable to isolate them, it's best to discard them rather than risking a houseful of insect-ridden plants.

GARDENERS' MOST-ASKED QUESTIONS

Q: Which herbs grow best indoors during the winter?
A: Try chive, basil, thyme, rosemary, oregano, sweet marjoram, mint and sage on a sunny kitchen windowsill.

Q: Which herbs make the most effective companion plants?
A: See Herbal Helpers (page 29), for a listing of those that are most effective. Companion planting may enhance flavor, repel insects or discourage diseases.

Q: Are any herbs poisonous?
A: Many herbs are poisonous. Never use herbs as an alternative to medicine without the advice of a qualified physician. Among the most toxic herbs when taken internally are castor bean, comfrey, *Digitalis*, pennyroyal, pokeweed, rue and tansy.

Q: Can herbs be combined with other plants?
A: Yes, they can be excellent companion plants and blend in well in the mixed border with bulbs, perennials and annuals. See Herbs in Harmony (pages 10–11) and Winning Plant Combinations (page 17).

Q: Is lavender hardy in New York?
A: Lavender is marginally hardy in Zone 6. It should be given extra winter protection in New York City and Philadelphia and surrounding areas. Plant in an area not exposed to winter winds and apply a winter mulch after the ground freezes. It will not winter over well much farther north.

Q: I am having trouble growing lavender from seed. Is it difficult?
A: Lavender isn't easy to grow from seed, which takes from three to four weeks to germinate at a soil temperature of 65° to 75°F. We recommend starting seeds inside, to ensure controlled conditions. Lavender needs a well-drained soil with a pH of 6.5 to 7.5. Try Burpee's new 'Early Flowering' lavender.

Q: Is rosemary hardy in New York City?
A: Marginally; if temperatures drop below 10°F, you can bring your rosemary inside in fall to winter over indoors.

Q: Which herbs are best for drying?

A: Most herbs used for cooking can be dried, including basil, bay, dill, sweet marjoram, oregano, rosemary, sage, tarragon and thyme.

Q: How should I dry my herbs?
A: Cut the herb on a sunny morning, tie the stems loosely in bunches and hang them upside down in a dry, dark location with good air circulation.

Q: Do herbs have fewer insect and disease problems than vegetables?
A: Some herbs appear to be natural insect repellents and are used as companion plants for this reason. Beyond this they are neither more nor less likely to experience pest and disease problems than other garden plants. Space them properly, rotate annual herbs, diversify your crops and grow the proper plants in the proper areas, and insect and disease problems should not be too troublesome.

Q: Can I use herbs safely for medicinal purposes?
A: NEVER use herbs to replace medicines without the advice of a qualified physician.

These ladies were busy answering the many inquiries received by W. Atlee Burpee Company at the turn of the century.

Q: Which herbs are good for bathing in?

A: Herbs are used in bathing as stimulants, to soothe muscles and to make the bath water fragrant. For stimulants, use basil, bay, mint, rosemary, sage, savory and thyme. To soothe muscles, try bay, oregano and sage. For fragrance, add bay, clove, mint, rosemary and pennyroyal.

Q: Which herbs are best for teas?

A: Chamomile, mint, lemon balm, catnip and dandelion are recommended. Not all herbs are suitable for making teas, and some are poisonous. Again, always consult with a physician if you want to try something new.

Q: Which herbs have edible flowers?

A: Nasturtium, borage, *Viola*, *Calendula*, anise, hyssop, rose and many of the thymes.

Q: Are there health benefits to cooking with herbs?

A: Cooking with herbs often means that people can cut down on their salt intake, because herbs add so much flavor. Some have nutritional value, among them dandelion and chive.

Q: What is the difference between coriander and cilantro?

A: The botanical name for both is *Coriandrum sativum*. Coriander and cilantro are the same plant. The name "coriander" usually refers to the plant's seeds and leaves, whereas "cilantro" tends to refer to the leaves only.

Q: What is the difference between anise and anise hyssop?

A: Anise (*Pimpinella Anisum*) is an annual herb, the licorice-flavored leaves of which are used in salads, the seeds in cakes and breads. Anise hyssop (*Agastache Foeniculum*) is a perennial herb, the leaves of which are used as a seasoning and for teas; the lavender flowers are edible.

Q: What is the difference between common chive and garlic chive?

A: Common chive (*Allium Schoenoprasum*) has grasslike foliage with a mild onion flavor, and grows to 12 to 18 inches. Garlic chive (*A. tuberosum*) has broader leaves and a flavor more like garlic; it grows to about 18 to 24 inches.

Q: What is the difference between German and Roman chamomile?

A: German chamomile (*Matricaria recutita*) is an annual that grows to 2 to 3 feet tall; the small, white daisylike flowers are used in teas. Roman chamomile (*Anthemis nobilis*) is not a true chamomile, grows to about 9 inches and is a perennial. Its small, white daisylike flowers are also used in teas and in potpourri.

Q: What is the difference between upland cress, watercress and garden cress?

A: Watercress (*Nasturtium officinale*) grows in such wet locations as streambeds, and matures about 50 days after planting. It is a perennial. Upland cress (*Barbarea verna*) is the dry-land equivalent of watercress; it matures in about 10 days and is an annual. Garden cress (*Lepidium sativum*) is a dry-land cress that can also be grown indoors easily. Cultivars of garden cress include curly-cress and salad cress.

Q: Will dill grow indoors?

A: Dill can grow to 3 feet tall and so doesn't lend itself to kitchen windowsill gardening. Burpee has a new variety of dill called 'Fern Leaf', more compact and ideal for growing indoors with plenty of light.

Q: What is the difference between Florence fennel and fennel?

A: Florence fennel (*Foeniculum vulgare dulce*) is also called sweet anise or *finocchio*, and is an annual. It is related to celery, and has feathery leaves and a licorice-flavored bulb at the base. Fennel (*F. vulgare* or *F. officinale*) doesn't form a bulb and is a perennial.

Q: How does Greek oregano differ from ordinary oregano?

A: Greek oregano (*Origanum vulgare*) has medicinal properties and produces small pink flowers excellent for drying. *O. hirtum* is the strong flavoring used in cooking.

Q: Why is my Greek oregano seed this year smaller than last year?

A: The size of seed depends on the cultural conditions under which the plants were produced while the seed formed. Smaller seeds don't necessarily produce smaller plants.

Q: Is the root of parsley edible?
A: The root of Hamburg or parsnip-rooted parsley is edible and is used to flavor soups and stews.

Q: Is safflower the same as saffron?
A: Safflower (*Carthamus tinctorius*) is an annual that produces thistlelike flowers, used in the production of an orange-yellow dye. Saffron is produced from the fall-blooming crocus (*Crocus sativus*), from the stigmata.

Q: What is the difference between summer and winter savory?
A: Summer savory (*Satureja hortensis*) is an annual. Winter savory (*S. montana*) is a hardy perennial. Winter savory is shorter, growing to 6 to 12 inches, and summer savory grows to about 12 inches. Both are used in cooking.

Please write or call for a free Burpee catalog:

W. Atlee Burpee & Company
300 Park Avenue
Warminster, PA 18974

(215) 674-9633

THE USDA PLANT HARDINESS MAP OF THE UNITED STATES

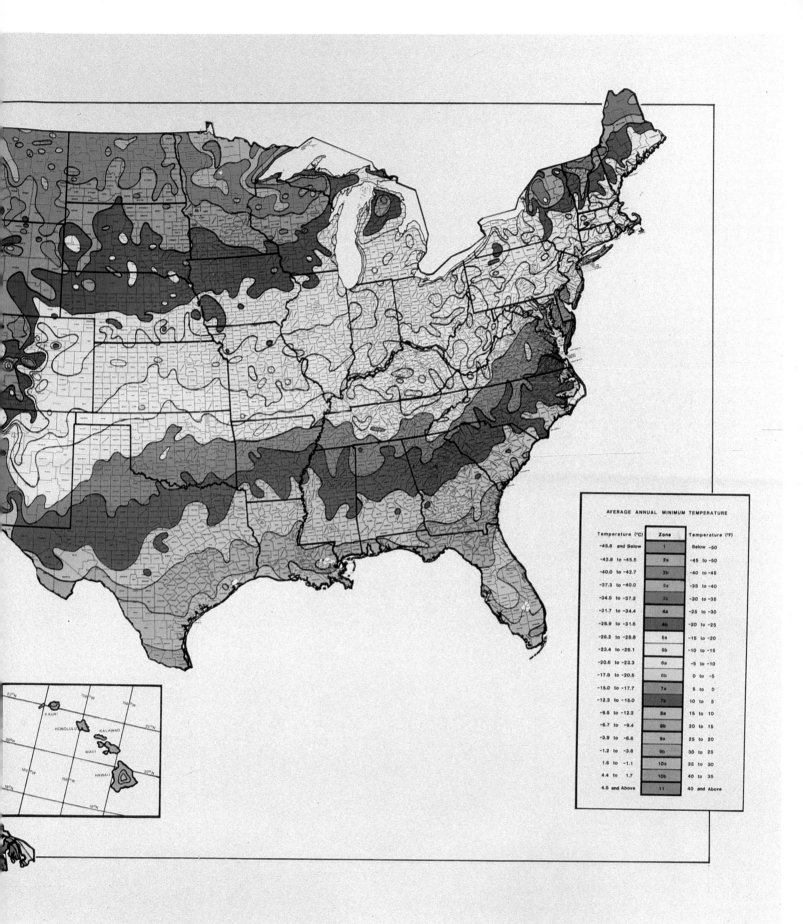

AVERAGE ANNUAL MINIMUM TEMPERATURE		
Temperature (°C)	Zone	Temperature (°F)
-45.6 and Below	1	Below -50
-42.8 to -45.5	2a	-45 to -50
-40.0 to -42.7	2b	-40 to -45
-37.3 to -40.0	3a	-35 to -40
-34.5 to -37.2	3b	-30 to -35
-31.7 to -34.4	4a	-25 to -30
-28.9 to -31.6	4b	-20 to -25
-26.2 to -28.8	5a	-15 to -20
-23.4 to -26.1	5b	-10 to -15
-20.6 to -23.3	6a	-5 to -10
-17.8 to -20.5	6b	0 to -5
-15.0 to -17.7	7a	5 to 0
-12.3 to -15.0	7b	10 to 5
-9.5 to -12.2	8a	15 to 10
-6.7 to -9.4	8b	20 to 15
-3.9 to -6.6	9a	25 to 20
-1.2 to -3.8	9b	30 to 25
1.6 to -1.1	10a	35 to 30
4.4 to 1.7	10b	40 to 35
4.5 and Above	11	40 and Above

INDEX

(NOTE: Italicized page numbers refer to captions)